Vintage is a word, usually with positive associations, that can describe anything from clothing and posters to watches and cars. In the world of wine—one of the few collectibles that's consumable—the vintage refers to the year grapes are harvested, and that vintage always tells a story. You can look up the weather in any almanac, but beyond that, some stories are known only to insiders—until now.

Grant Reynolds, award-winning sommelier and founder of Parcelle, deciphers these four-digit numerical signatures to reveal the impact of marketing and mentorship, technology and trends, and influencers old and new. Beginning in the late eighteenth century with a story about Thomas Jefferson's secret White House stash and spanning a quarter of a millennium to social media's effect on chenin blanc's popularity, *The Wine List* explores both the chemistry and sociology that have made vintages taste a certain way, fetch a certain price, or go extinct altogether. Read about the subpar bottling liquidated into coq au vin, the first winery to open after Prohibition, how "smooth" the Italians really are, and how an epic frost turned into a one-time-only joint venture.

Peppered throughout are sidebars on bigger ideas, like the taste of climate change and a dozen options better than pinot grigio, as well as useful references, such as which importers are most trustworthy and who's making actually good natural wine. Featuring mini timelines that capture significant historical moments within each vintage, and accompanied by unique, collage-style illustration, these entries solidify the idea that every bottle is a product of a particular moment in time. From the Founding Bottles (prewar) to Generation Old School (postwar to 1989) to the Reign of Points (1990 to 2008) and the Curious Age (2009 to present), Reynolds offers a full-bodied exploration of our changing tastes. Consider *The Wine List* your guide to discerning which wines are worthy of fame and which ones are just meant to keep your glass half full.

THE WINE LIST

THE WINE LIST

*Stories and Tasting Notes behind the
World's Most Remarkable Bottles*

GRANT
REYNOLDS

Assisted by Becky Cooper
Illustrations by Joan Wong

UNION
SQUARE
& CO.

NEW YORK

For Ned Benedict

*If you'd written this
book, it would be
smarter and funnier.
Thank you for sharing
so much with us.*

CONTENTS

9   *Introduction*

PART I

THE FOUNDING BOTTLES (PREWAR)

17   1787: America's First Wine Snob
18   1811: Comet Sipper
20   *A Closet Isn't a Cellar: Wine Storage*
23   1855: Napoleon Makes It (Too) Simple
24   1877: López and the Pest
26   *The Drunk Bug: Phylloxera*
29   1900: Margaux's Mammoth Moment
30   1905: A Partying Paris
32   *Perfecting the Blend: Multi-Vintage Wine*
35   1919: A Jockey and His Horse
36   1920: The Cool Clos
38   *You're the Only One: Single-Vineyard Wine*
41   1921: Dom Pérignon's First Pop
42   1929: Gone with the Gaudichots
45   1931: Pride and Port
46   *Sweet as Sugar: Dessert Wine*
48   1934: Prohibitively Riche
50   *That Hurt: The Impact of Prohibition*
53   1937: Better than Cooking Wine
54   1940: California's First Star

PART II

GENERATION OLD SCHOOL (POSTWAR TO 1989)

61   1945: One in Six Hundred
62   *Age Is Just a Number: Old Wine*
64   1947: Wrong Bank, Right Wine
67   1949: Bigger Isn't Always Better
68   1951: Australia's Debut Album
71   1955: On a Mission
72   1958: Big Bartolo Energy
74   *Aging Like Balthazar: Bottle Sizes*
76   1959: The Royal Family of Wine
79   1961: Better Days
80   1964: Back in the SSR
83   1966: Mondavi Slaps
84   1967: That Gaja Guy
87   1968: Something Super's Happening Here
88   *Under the Tuscan Sun: Super Tuscans*
90   1969: New Gigs Gone Right
93   1970: It Needs More Time
94   1971: A Time for White Wine
97   1973: Chardonnay Sauce
98   1974: A Bad Year's Best Bottle
101   1976: From Roots to Riches
102   1977: The Chianti Classic
105   1978: The Perfect Flight
106   1979: Two Pierres, One Montrachet
108   *The Food and Wine Police: Wine Laws*
111   1981: The Birth of Better Beaujolais
112   *Sulf-n-Pepa: Sulfur in Wine*
114   1982: And the Winner Is . . .
117   1983: When Being Late Is a Good Thing
118   1984: Pinot Goes West

120 *Next to Nike: Oregon Pinot Noir*
123 1985: I Knew You When
124 1986: The Start of Selosse's Something
126 *Trust Me: Importers to Know*
127 1988: The Beginning of the End
131 1989: If You Smell What Haut-Brion Is Cooking

PART III
THE REIGN OF POINTS (1990 TO 2008)

137 1990: Grand and Graceful
138 *Baby Got Blanc: Northern Rhône White Wine*
140 1991: Leroy Means Business
142 *Moon Cycles and Manure: Biodynamic Wine*
145 1992: Stars Are Born
146 1994: California Love
149 1996: Come Si Dice "Orange"? Gravner.
150 *What's Old Is New Again: Orange Wine*
152 1997: Smooooooth
155 2001: The Underground
157 *Water Wine: Pinot Grigio*
158 2002: La Romanée Reboot
161 2003: Hot Rods
163 2004: That's Dark
165 *The Taste of Heat: Climate Change*
166 *The Good Die Young: White Wine's Aging Problem*
168 2006: Down the Drain
171 2008: It's What's Inside That Counts

PART IV
THE CURIOUS AGE (2009 TO PRESENT)

177 2009: Sister Act
178 *The B-Side: Burgundy's New Producers*
180 2010: Chablis and Charlemagne
183 2012: #CheninCheninChenin
185 *What Does It Mean? Natural Wine*
187 2013: Burlotto Boosts Barolo
188 *Protect the North: Alto Piemonte*
190 2016: The Unlucky Seven
193 2017: Celebrating the French Underdogs
195 *No Way: Rosé*
197 2018: Meunier Makes the Team
198 2020: Spain Sings

200 *Acknowledgments*
202 *References and Further Learning*
203 *Index*

INTRODUCTION

"Vintage" is a word—almost always with positive associations—that can be used to describe everything from clothing and posters to watches and cars. In my world, it's the year grapes are harvested—the foundation for every bottle of wine. The unique expression of a specific bottle of wine is defined by a few basic constants: the type of grape or grapes used, the place (country, region, vineyard) where those grapes were grown, and the producer or winemaker's technical decisions in turning those grapes into wine. The most common differentiator of a vintage is the weather of that year, but the four numbers on a bottle can be about a lot more than that. The numerical signature can be a discreet mark of distinction, or, in select years, a more ostentatious declaration of quality and financial value.

Even before I was legally allowed to drink—in America, at least—I fell in love with wine. This was for two reasons: 1) I liked to party, and 2) I truly loved the stuff—the history, the taste, and everything that came along with it. I spent a year of high school in Italy, and I drank whatever was on the table. When I began to deeply care about what I was drinking, I was working at a restaurant called Frasca Food and Wine in Boulder, Colorado, with two of my early mentors, sommeliers Matthew Mather and Bobby Stuckey. These guys would drop names I'd never heard before (and definitely couldn't pronounce), like Rayas, Gaja, and Dauvissat, with a joy deeper than most people speak of their loved ones. Their passion sparked my own. Working in a restaurant was tough, but the access to wines I never in my lifetime would have been able to afford made the long hours and high stress inconsequential. I was in the fortunate position of being able to consume wines older than I was. It's said that the best wine palates of today belong to people who have worked on restaurant floors, and this is why.

At this time, circa 2008, "good wine" was still viewed as stuffy rather than cool, but I didn't care. I was transfixed by the science, stories, sagas, and lore that made a certain wine taste a certain way or made it wildly expensive or even extinct. I learned everything I could from the few important books on the subject, exceptional mentors, an addiction to researching decades-old weather reports, and the early internet. I typed into Google: "What was the weather like in Italy in 1988?" My birth year. I had been told by several famous winemakers and master sommeliers that it was a good but not great vintage in Barolo. The best year of Sassicaia. A terrible one in Burgundy, with the exception of some whites. Magic for Roumier. A heroic time for Champagne, but only the ones made from 100 percent chardonnay. A vintage for spectacular examples of riesling. Reds of the Northern Rhône in the shadows of '89 and '90, but possibly better. Not a bad year for the pre-Parker style of California cabernet. But far from sating my curiosity, what I discovered only piqued my interest further. I found myself on a quest to find out why all those things were true about 1988—and how just those four digits could say so much.

THE MOST COMMON DIFFERENTIATOR OF A VINTAGE IS THE WEATHER OF THAT YEAR, BUT THE FOUR NUMBERS ON A BOTTLE CAN BE ABOUT A LOT MORE THAN THAT.

I saved up my pennies to travel abroad, where I could drink more wine and work for free. I was taken in at places like Roscioli in Rome, where I first discovered the aging potential of obscure Italian grapes like fiano, aglianico, and frappato. I picked grapes at one of the most exceptional (and welcoming) wineries in the world, Domaine Dujac, where I learned that if restaurant work is grueling, picking grapes in Burgundy is the industry's most severe corporal punishment. At Dujac, I tasted wines from the 1950s and '60s for the first time. I didn't yet have a concept of their value, which, in hindsight, enabled me to experience them in a humbler manner.

After I'd tried the best bottles of the classic French producers from Bordeaux to Burgundy and the Rhône at Dujac, I signed up to work, again for free, at René Redzepi's Noma in Copenhagen. Natural wine was just beginning to make its way beyond the bars of Paris. At Noma, I tasted the good and the bad of this controversial category. The wine director at the time, Mads Kleppe, had (and has) exceptional access, taste, and a disciplined point of view on which wines should be served at what was then the best restaurant in the world. Mads championed underdogs that today have become collectibles. Wines from producers like Overnoy, Prévost, Sébastien Riffault, Métras, Pfifferling, Bernaudeau, and so many others were available by the glass on any given night.

Then, in 2012, I moved to New York City. Rajat Parr, a sommelier on the short list of people who have tasted the most valuable bottles in the world, encouraged me to go to get access to an abundance of old and rare wines. That prompt was reason enough for me. My usher into this exclusive world was Robert Bohr, a guy who, like Rajat, has consumed a ton of great wine. Robert sold me on the idea of opening a casual food spot with extraordinary wine instead of the more obvious career move of taking a sommelier position at a highly rated restaurant like Eleven Madison Park or Daniel. That restaurant, in the heart of the West Village, was Charlie Bird, and it went on to earn a number of accolades for its wine list. Together, and along with an amazing group, Robert and I would open two more restaurants celebrating that same ethos: really good food, even better wine—and you can wear sneakers if you want to. As the wine director of and a partner in some of the best wine destinations in the greatest city on Earth, I'd open bottles older than my parents, savoring the small sips afforded to sommeliers, knowing it might be the only time I'd ever smell that wine, let alone have a glass. I learned to be critical of trophy bottles that simply aren't that exciting, and to celebrate the cheap, delicious ones that I'd take home and hoard for myself.

All of this is to say: I'm really lucky. As I get older, and as wines get older alongside me, we've all gotten a little bit softer, quieter with time. Some wines blossom into better versions of themselves, and some just hang on for dear life. But what determines a wine's destiny? I find myself on the same quest I started at the beginning of my career: to understand how the combination of facts and events in the year a wine was conceived—its vintage—impacts not only how a wine tastes, but also how it lasts.

The Wine List is, well, my wine list: an accounting of what I believe to be the most remarkable vintages—a few spectacular, many excellent, and even a handful so bad they've earned mention in the annals of history. You'll find in-world gossip, tales of the most famous vintages with accompanying insight into whether that fame is deserved or just hype, and overviews of the next generation of producers who will soon become legends in their own right. You'll get a little history lesson, too. By asking producers many questions, visiting their cellars, in some cases even working their fields, reading the books, and drinking the wines (the best part), I have a distinct view of the wine world, past and present.

This book profiles notable vintages and then theorizes why and how these vintages became noteworthy. It also offers an introduction to the names and places that made those wines possible. It's broken into four parts: the pre–World War II icons that broke ground for many; the triumphant

WHILE OTHER FORMS OF ART ARE INEXTRICABLE FROM THE PERIOD OF THEIR CREATION, WINE, IN AN EVEN MORE LITERAL WAY, IS THE PRODUCT OF A PARTICULAR MOMENT IN TIME.

bottles and people who, following the war, crafted many of today's most respected wines; the first era impacted by both climate change and designing for the global market; and, finally, today's age that caters to the most curious, diverse, and enthusiastic consumers in wine history so far. Along the way, we'll pause to shine a light on some bigger ideas, like great labels and what biodynamic farming actually is. And so you don't have to filter through old tabloids and weather reports to know what happened in, say, Eastern France in 1969, each entry—representing one vintage—points to some wonderful, significant, and even bizarre moments within that year, separate from the world of wine. With research by bestselling author and former *New Yorker* staffer Becky Cooper, you'll see that while other forms of art are inextricable from the period of their creation, wine, in an even more literal way, is the product of a particular moment in time.

The Wine List answers the question of why we have come to classify certain vintages the way we do. And above all, it reminds us that just like the wine, all things change—for better and for worse.

PART I

THE FOUNDING BOTTLES (PREWAR)

he origins of wine have been recorded as early as 6000 BCE in places like Georgia, Iran, and Armenia. Back then, wine wasn't bottled, and it certainly wasn't collected. I'm also assuming there were no tasting notes, no wine dinners, and no connoisseurs. It was just alcohol made from grapes. Later, vine cuttings traveled the same way that spices, plants, and animals did when the world was colonized by the Greeks, Romans, Portuguese, and British. Fast-forward several thousand years and transform it into something that sits at the intersection of art and industry, and you'll arrive at wine as we know it today: a glass bottle most often filled with 750 milliliters of fermented grape juice, labeled with some art and standardized legal requirements, and topped with a stopper.

The first hints of the commercialization of wine began around the sixteenth century, when wine regions adjacent to ports like Bordeaux and Madeira began to market their product. This is the point at which labels specific to wineries—and to a notion of quality—began to emerge. Inherent to the label was the idea that the name of a château, or a family's house, could convey a specific indication of quality. Wine was a luxury even then.

In the Age of Enlightenment, science took hold, commerce went international, and the agricultural revolution dramatically increased the productivity of farms and fields. New glass technology meant wine could travel farther and stay fresh longer, and demand for libations that could last on monthslong transatlantic journeys shaped the global palate.

From the 1700s until World War II, the wine trade was dominated by Bordeaux and the sweet wines like port, Sauternes, and Madeira. Bottles were also produced in Italy, Spain, and California, but they were largely consumed locally until the turn of the eighteenth century. These lesser-known areas had only just started to emerge when the catastrophic phylloxera outbreak threatened to end the wine industry (see page 26). Alas, other bumps in the road lay ahead— World War I, the Great Depression, and Prohibition.

The stories that follow focus on controversy, tragedy, and destiny-shaping environmental events, and spotlight the wineries that triumphed despite these challenges to form the foundation of wine, and the wine industry, as we know it today.

AMERICA'S FIRST WINE SNOB

UNFORTUNATELY, NO RECORD EXISTS DETAILING WHEN EXACTLY collecting wine became Wine Collecting. While some of Europe's best-known wineries date back to the eleventh century, wine was only considered slightly more "high society" than beer—i.e., by no means something to be infatuated with, other than for its physical effects. The man to change that, in America at least, was none other than the Francophile Founding Father, Thomas Jefferson. During his tenure as ambassador to France from 1785 to 1789, America's first wine collector and enthusiast shipped bottles back to the White House, where a concise collection, paid for by the people, still exists.

The man had great taste. Many of the wines he sent home are still considered the fundamental bottles of wine collecting—Bordeaux, port, and Sauternes, forever favored for their flavors' glacial evolution. But Jefferson isn't only associated with being the world's first wine influencer; he's also at the heart of the single most notorious bottle ever sold.

In 1985, at an auction in London, a bottle of 1787 Château Lafite went up for sale—a bottle with the initials TH.J etched into the glass. Legend has it that before shipping wines back home, Jefferson requested that his signature be adhered to the bottles, presumably as a way to keep less distinguished members of the cabinet away from the good stuff. This 1787 Château Lafite fetched £105,000 (about £300,000 today), which was the highest auction price ever for a wine at the time. Wine hadn't yet reached the range of consumers or prices it achieves today, so a six-figure sale was big news. The Forbes family, who bought the bottle, purchased it not to drink but as an artifact of national significance.

Following this sale, other signed Jefferson bottles were traded as well, including more 1787 Lafite(s). Fast-forward twenty years: Bill Koch, a buyer of some of those bottles, sought authentication of the TH.J signature in preparation for an exhibition of antiques at the Boston Museum of Fine Art. When the Thomas Jefferson Foundation, contacted to verify the bottles, declared that the bottles had not, in fact, belonged to the former president, they ignited the biggest scandal the wine world had ever seen.

Real or not, with bottles this old and rare, we can't help but wonder: What would it have tasted like? Had it been stored in proper conditions, it could have been great—maybe even six figures great. Who knows. But like any collectible, its allure (and therefore its value) isn't just about the taste.

On May 13, British admiral Arthur Philip sets sail for Australia with the goal of establishing a penal colony. In addition to prisoners and crew, he brings the first vine cuttings to reach Australian soil. None survive the heat and humidity.

The next day—May 14—delegates begin arriving in Philadelphia for the Constitutional Convention. Delaware becomes the first state of the Union, followed by Pennsylvania and New Jersey.

Over in France, chemist Antoine Lavoisier is the first to suggest that silica, which had been used to make glass for at least four thousand years, might be an oxide of a hitherto unknown element, silicon.

1787

COMET SIPPER

IN THE EARLY 1800S, WINE WAS LARGELY SOLD IN JUGS OR OTHER LARGE vessels, and it wasn't meant for aging beyond the journey from vineyard to drinking glass. Thankfully, there were a few exceptions. When a properly stored bottle from this era is found, it is extraordinary to even the least-discerning palate.

Some of the world's most age-worthy wines are the sweet or dessert wines from France, Spain, Portugal, Germany, and Hungary. High sugar levels do double duty as a preservative. If you have a sweet tooth, you'll find no greater bottle to end a meal than a bottle of Sauternes from Château d'Yquem. It's a "wine" in the way that Marilyn Monroe is an "actress." And there is perhaps no greater vintage of it than the 1811.

So what happened in 1811? Well, during the October harvest, as the ripe, honeyed grapes were being picked, the Great Comet of 1811 shot across the sky. An old farmers' tale says that wines made from grapes harvested during a celestial event are always of exceptional quality. Like ocean tides and the beach, the moon and stars seem to have a direct impact on wine—though winemakers are happy to leave the precise mechanisms of cosmic influence a mystery.

That said, while the celestial event might have had something to do with 1811 Yquem, the cosmos can't take all the credit. Yquem has been a trophy wine for centuries, lauded for its caramel color, creamy texture, and confectionery taste. In the wine classification of 1855 (see page 23), Yquem was the only Sauternes given the highest rating, indicating its perceived superiority over all other wines of its type.

On January 8, Charles Deslondes leads one of the largest slave revolts in US history—an uprising of more than two hundred near New Orleans.

After Napoleon yanks the crown off the Spanish king and plops it onto his own brother's head in 1808, no one can agree on who rules Spain or its territories. Battles for sovereignty spread across Latin America this year.

If revolutions are in the air, steamships are in the water. On October 11, the first steam-powered ferry service begins transporting passengers between New York City and Hoboken, New Jersey.

1811

A CLOSET ISN'T A CELLAR: WINE STORAGE

What's the point in obsessing over winemaking if you don't also care about making it last? The key is in how you store it. Wine needs a dark, stable environment with some humidity. Oxygen is the enemy. Nowadays, people even put their wine on the blockchain to assure collectors decades in the future that the wine has been stored well. But this level of attention is a modern phenomenon.

For thousands of years, clay was king. In China, archaeological evidence of the oldest fermented beverage—a grape and rice wine dating to 7000 BCE—was found on pottery shards. In Georgia, where winemaking was established during the Neolithic period, there's evidence of storage in enormous clay vessels buried in the ground. The Egyptians, Greeks, and Romans mostly kept their wine in terra-cotta jars of varying sizes—Homer is reputed to have had a collection lined up by year. Clay was good at keeping its contents fresh, especially when stoppered with cork—but it fell out of favor when the Roman Empire expanded to Gaul. There, it was discovered that the ancient French (who were predominantly interested in beer-making) used wooden barrels to store their wares. These were stronger, lighter, and more portable than clay amphorae. Unfortunately, wood is much worse than clay at keeping oxygen out. So by the first century CE, when clay's dominance came to an end, so did the ability to store wines for longer than a year. (One exception was sweet wines, whose high sugar content acted as a natural preservative [see page 46].)

That all slowly started to change in the 1600s in England, when wine finally met coal-fired glass. Coal heats to higher temperatures than wood, allowing for stronger, more durable glass. Cork also made a reappearance. The first mention of a corkscrew appears in 1681 in a museum catalog: "a Steel Worme used for the drawing of Corks out of Bottles." Even then, ensuring a stable temperature for shipping across the world was impossible until refrigerated shipping containers debuted in the late 1960s.

What does the future of wine storage hold? Possibly moving away from the cork and glass that made this new age of vintage wines possible. Cork taint affects as many as one in thirty bottles, so scientists have begun experimenting with alternative cork closures called Diam, which come with the guarantee of being fungus-free. Glass has gotten a bad rap because it takes so much energy to make and to ship, and bottles are often single-use. There's now a call to reserve glass for the small percentage of wine destined to be cellared—the vast majority is consumed within the first three years. For the rest of the stuff, there's a push to destigmatize boxed wine. (Cans are energy-intensive to produce, too.) At the very least, the tacky college version of yourself can say you were there first.

NAPOLEON MAKES IT (TOO) SIMPLE

THE WORLD OF WINE DOESN'T HAVE A KENTUCKY DERBY, WORLD CUP, or World Series. No Emmys, Grammys, or Oscars for us. In fact, we have no notable ranking of producers—aside from the list Emperor Napoleon III demanded in 1855. He was hosting a sort of world's fair in Paris, and he wanted to make France's best wines more approachable to foreign visitors, likely in an effort to build allure for the international market. It proved a daunting task.

The Grand Cru Classés en 1855, or the Bordeaux Wine Official Classification of 1855, was both controversial and highly influential, and it remains so even today. The best wines from the primary region of Bordeaux—the Left Bank, or Médoc—were ranked by a group of local wine brokers. They had no scorecard or set criteria to judge by but instead pooled their collective knowledge on the quality and the marketability of the wineries to determine which would be worthy of classification from level 1 (the top) to level 5 (the bottom). The producers deemed the best of the best would be labeled "Premiers Crus," or First Growths; the list then moves from Second Growth down to Fifth Growth. Allegedly, they pulled this list together in only a few weeks before releasing the classification that still stands today.

Wines still fetch prices according to their 1855 classifications, even if the quality is not always consistent with their rankings. Many of those top wineries have been sold or have wavered in quality, and some likely weren't all that good to begin with. The reverse is also true: there is collective agreement by collectors and the market that some wines belong in higher categories. What's more, many of the best producers of Bordeaux are entirely unclassified. The list only took into account one part of Bordeaux, and it has never been updated to include any new producers. Alas, a reset of the classification is not happening, so the cumulative effect is variations in the market that essentially negate Napoleon's intention of letting the world know, without question, which Bordeaux are the best.

At the same event that gives birth to Napoleon's VIP list of Bordeaux, bars of aluminum—rarer and more expensive than gold at the time—are displayed next to the French crown jewels.

Massachusetts becomes the first state to issue a school vaccine mandate.

Welsh astronomer Thereza Llewelyn produces some of the earliest photographs of the moon.

1855

Bordeaux producers omitted from the 1855 ranking that have had success regardless are:

- Château Ausone
- Château Cheval Blanc
- Château Clinet
- Château l'Eglise-Clinet
- Château L'Évangile
- Château La Conseillante
- Château La Mission Haut-Brion
- Château Lafleur
- Château Le Pin
- Château Petrus
- Château Trotanoy
- Vieux Château Certan

LÓPEZ AND THE PEST

IN 1877, A PEST CALLED PHYLLOXERA WAS RAVAGING THE VINEYARDS of France and, before long, the rest of Europe. The wine industry was in shambles, and the threat of wine-pocalypse quickly accelerated from plausible to imminent. It forced the players in major wine regions like Bordeaux to source grapes from places they would have never thought of simply to survive. Most were turning to less prestigious parts of France when a young Chilean student named Rafael López de Heredia found some unaffected vines in the Spanish region of Rioja. For a time, Rioja became a source of grapes for a very desperate France. But López de Heredia knew he had found more than just a short-term fix to a problem, and he turned it into an opportunity to build one of the most significant wineries in the world.

The López de Heredia winery is a sprawling network of both century-old and contemporary buildings that embody Don Rafael's mission to make Spanish wine that rivals or even surpasses that of the French. Though his vines, like the rest of Rioja's, eventually succumbed to phylloxera and needed to be replanted, the brand is known for its unwavering commitment to the style that Don Rafael crafted before the pest arrived, including aging the wines in oak barrels for up to ten years (the norm in France is only two). This time gives the wine flavors more akin to tea and cigars than to flowers and fruit. López de Heredia's wines are also famous for their ability to age for decades in bottle—some believe the wine's exposure to oxygen while aging in oak barrels inoculates the wine against oxygen in the bottle. Now Rioja as a whole is widely considered one of the world's best wine regions, and under the stewardship of his great-granddaughters, López de Heredia consistently sweeps the podium of the region's best wines. Drinking López de Heredia's Rioja evokes a long-gone era—it's the wine equivalent to walking through the ruins of Pompeii, or at least through the hills of Rioja in the time before phylloxera.

It's a good year for art and innovation: Tchaikovsky's *Swan Lake* debuts, Tolstoy publishes the final section of *Anna Karenina,* and Alexander Graham Bell installs the first commercial telephone service.

On March 1, Frederick Douglass becomes a US Marshal—marking the first time a Black American is confirmed by the Senate for a presidential appointment.

The British finally repeal the tax that had been levied on newspapers since 1712. In its absence, "reading all about it" becomes much more accessible—and media flourishes.

1877

THE DRUNK BUG: PHYLLOXERA

The epidemic that nearly brought an end to winemaking in Europe began in 1862 when a wine merchant named Monsieur Borty received a shipment of vine cuttings from America and planted them in his Rhône vineyard. The march of death was slow at first: only a cluster of vines a few kilometers away were infected the first summer, then, a year later, Borty's own vines started to shrivel. (All of them, except, mysteriously, the American imports.) By 1865, the affliction had spread to nearby towns. *Something* was rotten, to be sure. Soon, millions of acres of France's vineyards were destroyed, and winemakers became desperate to stop the wretched illness. They resorted to increasingly drastic and expensive poisons. Some burned their fields. Thousands fled the country. None of it worked. Instead, the problem spread even farther, to Spain, then to Italy and beyond. Panicked, the French minister of agriculture issued a sizable reward for anyone who could find a cure.

Charles Valentine Riley, Missouri's state entomologist, didn't need the financial incentive to become obsessed. He had spent a good part of his childhood in France and hated to think of the countryside being destroyed. In 1869, he determined that the most likely culprit was phylloxera: a microscopic aphid that attacks roots and feasts on leaves. Native to the East Coast of the United States, it had spread across the country with the pioneers, then hitched a ride over the Atlantic in the package destined for Monsieur Borty. From there, the aphids hid in the soil, reproduced like mad, and spread on machinery, contaminated plant material, and even footwear. A fierce proponent of Darwin's new theory of evolution, the Missourian hypothesized that the culprit might also be the cure, as North American vines had coevolved with the pest and had developed a resistance to it over time. So he and a few other botanists suggested that winemakers graft their old vines onto resistant American stock.

Needless to say, many winemakers were horrified at the prospect of decapitating their beloved ancient vines only to suture them onto inferior American bases. Imagine a vintage Chanel suit finished off with durable Walmart shoes. But facing the complete decimation of their livelihoods, French winemakers had no choice. Experiments began in Southern France, and by 1895, more than a third of all French vines had been Frankensteined onto American roots. Champagne, one of the last French regions to be hit, was nearly fully grafted by 1920. (By the way, the French minister

refused to award the prize to anyone, saying the solution was a workaround rather than a cure.)

In today's Europe, Cyprus, Santorini, and the Canary Islands remain untouched by phylloxera, and a few precious pockets of ungrafted vines still exist on the mainland (see Pride and Port, page 45). No one knows the exact existing acreage, but if you see "Vieilles Vignes" or "Vigne Vecchie" on a wine's label, it's a sure sign that what's inside the bottle is OG. Bollinger has two plots of pinot noir that resisted the plague, and from them, the winery makes the most sought-after Champagne: Vieilles Vignes Françaises. (They had three plots, but the third succumbed to phylloxera in 2004—a stark reminder that the pest is far from eradicated.) These old vines, these survivors, should be treasured as the national monuments they are.

MARGAUX'S MAMMOTH MOMENT

AT THE DAWN OF THE TWENTIETH CENTURY, FINE WINE WAS STILL ALL about Bordeaux. Champagne was only just beginning to take itself seriously; Burgundy was focused on making wine in bulk; and the Rhône was selling some of its syrah to wealthier Bordeaux properties whose vintages lacked volume and flavor. So when France wanted to celebrate the new century with a bottle that had the flash and stature to keep it in the top spot for another hundred years, Château Margaux was a shoo-in for the task. By 1900, this Bordeaux legend had been in business for around four hundred years—with distinctions including the first wine ever auctioned (1771), a winery comparable to the splendor of Versailles (built in 1810), and a top slot in the 1855 classification (see page 23).

Landmark vintages have a built-in marketability, but even without that leg up, 1900 would still be the best Château Margaux vintage of all time. The weather yielded grapes with a rich and pronounced flavor. It was also the highest-volume vintage in more than eighty years, giving the château plenty of bottles to promote and distribute. Substantial quantity and the highest quality almost never align; an abundant crop can cause simplification in flavors—not dissimilar to the way in which any artisanal craft is diminished if it scales too much. But luckily for everyone, the 1900 vintage of Château Margaux is the rarest of the rare: a Rolls-Royce lacquered in gold, but produced as plentifully as a Ford F-150.

The first Michelin Guide, which included maps, instructions on how to change a tire, and where to stop for food, is compiled by the founders of Michelin Tires as a way to create demand for cars. (Only a few thousand vehicles exist in all of France at the time.)

New York City subway construction officially begins. The mayor ceremoniously breaks ground with a silver shovel and carries a clump of earth back to his office in his silk hat.

Global life expectancy reaches thirty-two years.

1900

A PARTYING PARIS

IF CHAMPAGNE HAS A YEAR LISTED, IT'S MORE PRESTIGIOUS AND expensive than those that don't. But these vintages are the exception. Most Champagne doesn't specify a year, meaning the bottle contains a blend of vintages, some good years and some less so. This way, no wine is wasted, while a baseline for quality is maintained.

But "good enough" wasn't good enough for Eugène-Aimé Salon, a bon vivant who grew up in Champagne and worked as a fur trader in the streets of Paris. Eugène was a Parisian socialite at the time when Matisse, Picasso, and others were partying in the city at the peak of the belle époque. Those celebratory times needed a great Champagne, and Eugène stepped up. He created the Champagne Salon in 1905, which, he vowed, would contain wines only from the best grapes and the best years. The first vintage is said to have been for friends and family only. He released the 1921 to the public (coincidentally the same year that its rival, Dom Pérignon, debuted as well).

To this day, Salon has stayed true to its philosophy. The grapes are from Mesnil—the Fifth Avenue of Champagne vineyards—and since its first release in 1905, no more than five bottles have come out of any decade. There's still no "good enough" when it comes to Salon—only spectacular.

Still working his day job at the Swiss patent office, Albert Einstein publishes four papers that transform our understanding of the universe, including, yes, the one containing $E=mc^2$. No pressure for that side hustle of yours.

Speaking of relativity, 1905 is either a good year or a bad one for dental surgery, depending on your proclivities. German chemist Alfred Einhorn synthesizes novocaine. Before that, the most commonly used local anesthetic was cocaine.

The first nickelodeon opens in Pittsburgh, Pennsylvania—its name combines the Greek word for "theater" and the price of admission—and soon nickel theaters take off around the country.

1905

PERFECTING THE BLEND: MULTI-VINTAGE WINE

If you're looking to buy Champagne and Salon is out of your price range, chances are you'll see MV or NV on the wine list, which stands for multi-vintage or non-vintage and means not all the grapes in that bottle were harvested in the same year. Before climate change, the Champagne region was chilly and unpredictable, so if producers wanted to make something every year, they needed to blend multiple vintages together to ensure volume and balanced flavors.

The logic is this: weather changes the taste of wine, which means that a vintage is the expression of that particular year's sultry summer, smoky skies, or torrential rains. Some years the wine will be juicy and jammy, others it will be unbalanced and acidic, and maybe, if you're lucky, a few will be perfect. For many, that variation is not only something to celebrate, it's the very reason for wine: each bottle is a time capsule. But what if you wanted something more consistent and more balanced? By showcasing deliberate winemaking choices for MV and NV bottlings, a producer can announce, "This is the taste of *my* ideal wine."

One blending technique sometimes used in Champagne is borrowed from the solera method, which Andalusian producers use to make sherry. In sherry-making, barrels are stacked on top of each other, with those containing the oldest stuff at the bottom and getting younger on the way up. Every time you draw from the bottom barrel, you replace what you took with the same amount from the barrel one row above, and so on up the chain. For Champagne, instead of a series of barrels, the reserve is normally stored in a single large tank. With either method, this perpetual collection technique gives even the youngest wine the mature complexity of much older vintages.

Though the weather's changing in the region, the vast majority—around 75 percent—of Champagne production is still NV. A few producers (Chris Howell in California, Vega Sicilia in Spain, and Valdivieso in Chile) have started experimenting with blending multiple vintages for still wines as well.

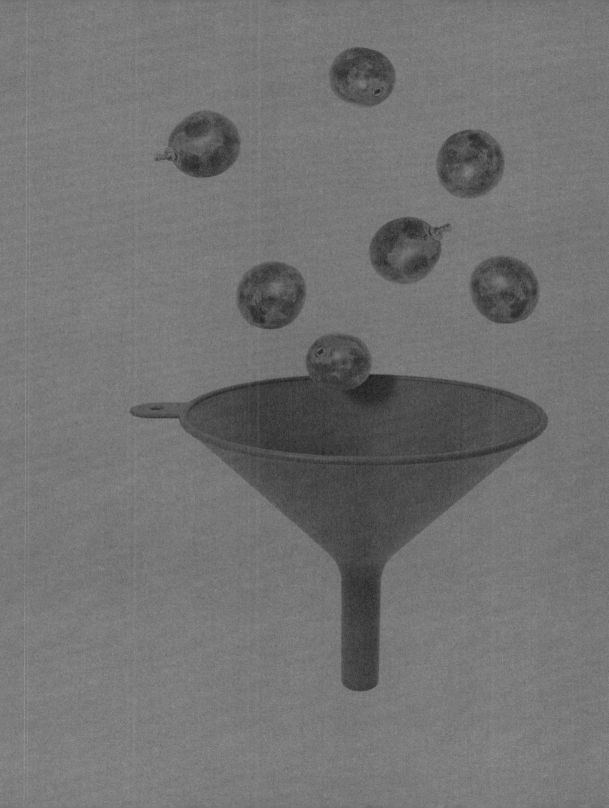

A JOCKEY AND HIS HORSE

A FEW FACTS TO KNOW ABOUT CHAMBERTIN:

It is the name of a vineyard in the northern part of France's Burgundy region.

The soil is primarily limestone.

The grape grown in the vineyard is pinot noir.

In total, its yield is around 60,000 bottles per year, which is tiny.

Napoleon couldn't get enough of those bottles.

And finally, if you retain no other information about this vineyard, remember that Domaine Armand Rousseau is and was its greatest-ever producer.

The Rousseau family name first adorned bottles of Chambertin in 1919. The labels read *Vieux Plantes*, which translates simply to "Old Plants." In this case, "old" doesn't signify a specific number of years, but rather is meant as a stamp of quality: the older the vines, the better the wine. The inclusion of this language was an early promotional effort by the family to make it known that *their* Chambertin was made from the best and oldest stuff—better than any others. And it was true. While Chambertin in general is an excellent vineyard, the Rousseau family has continuously steered its land—like a jockey and his horse—to greatness. In fact, you'll find virtually no losses.

Other vineyards attach the Chambertin name to their own. Some of these neighbors are of exceptional quality as well, but they have never been the main act. Those vineyards are:

- Chambertin-Clos de Bèze
- Chapelle-Chambertin
- Charmes-Chambertin
- Griotte-Chambertin
- Latricières-Chambertin
- Mazis-Chambertin
- Ruchottes-Chambertin

World leaders sign the Treaty of Versailles, officially ending World War I. The United States fails to ratify it.

President Woodrow Wilson establishes the Grand Canyon as a national park.

A wave of molasses traveling at 35 mph pours through a Boston neighborhood when a large storage tank explodes, killing twenty-one people. For decades following, on hot summer days, residents claim the area still smells like molasses.

1919

THE COOL CLOS

"IF THESE WALLS COULD TALK" IS A PHRASE COMMONLY UTTERED while reminiscing at an old bar or music venue with sticky floors. But instead of groupie gossip and tales of drunken escapades, the walls of the Clos des Ducs in Volnay tell its history through grapes. Clos des Ducs is a walled vineyard (*clos* means "closed" in French) with stone partitions documented as early as the 1500s. The walls were built to enclose land worthy of the specific distinction. Clos des Ducs belonged to the d'Angerville family for centuries, but the first vintage bottled under the family name was the 1920.

At the time, only a couple of other grape growers in Burgundy were bottling their own wines. Far more common was the practice of cooperative winemaking, in which farmers sold grapes to merchants known as négociants. These négociants handled the wine production—blending wine from multiple farmers—and sales of the final product, from which each farmer got a cut. Sem d'Angerville, Clos des Ducs's owner, stood up to Burgundy's ruling négociants and took a daring leap to make and sell wine under his family's seal instead of taking the easier—but less rewarding—path of selling wine to these merchants. Sem was confident in his family's land in Volnay, and the gamble paid off—eventually. While these wines now sell out every year upon release, it took nearly a century of commitment to the family land for that to be the case.

Following in his grandfather and father's footsteps of running the family winery, Guillaume d'Angerville has preserved the legacy of this land today. After a successful gig as a banker, he returned home to Volnay, which sits within the walls of the Clos des Ducs, to continue the craft of making some of Burgundy's gentlest and most soothing bottles of red wine.

When the clock strikes midnight on January 17, Prohibition begins in the United States. It won't officially end until 1933.

The Nineteenth Amendment is ratified, finally giving women the right to vote.

Alfred L. Cralle, inventor of the ice cream scoop, dies. His design is still in use today.

1920

YOU'RE THE ONLY ONE: SINGLE-VINEYARD WINE

The more specific a geographic region is on a wine label, the smaller the area the grapes came from, and, generally, the higher the quality of the wine. (If the wine label you're reading says "from EU grapes," maybe run the other way.) Most wines can be traced to a number of vineyards across a region. "Estate" or "Domaine" wines are made exclusively from grapes grown on vineyards that the winemaker owns, while "single-vineyard" wines like Clos des Ducs take this specificity to the next level: all grapes must come from a single plot of land whose boundaries are legally defined. They're pretty rare, but as interest in terroir has grown, so, too, have the number of single-vineyard wines.

These wines are the purest reflection of the idea that wine grown on slightly different pieces of land—with slightly different sun/water/wind exposure and drainage—will taste different.

Accordingly, they also reflect the belief that the raw material of the vineyard is something to be prized in its own right. Just as some apartments are more expensive simply because of their zip code, some wines are deemed fancier simply because of the land where their grapes were grown.

This belief—and pricing system—is foundational in Burgundy, where wine is classified according to land, not producer. The ranking of Burgundy vineyards into grands crus and premiers crus legally came into play in the 1930s, but the land had been categorized and named long before by fourteenth-century monks.

It is important to keep in mind, though, that ranking wine based on land doesn't take into account the quality of the winemaker. Let's just say the tragedy of making terrible wine from great grapes happens.

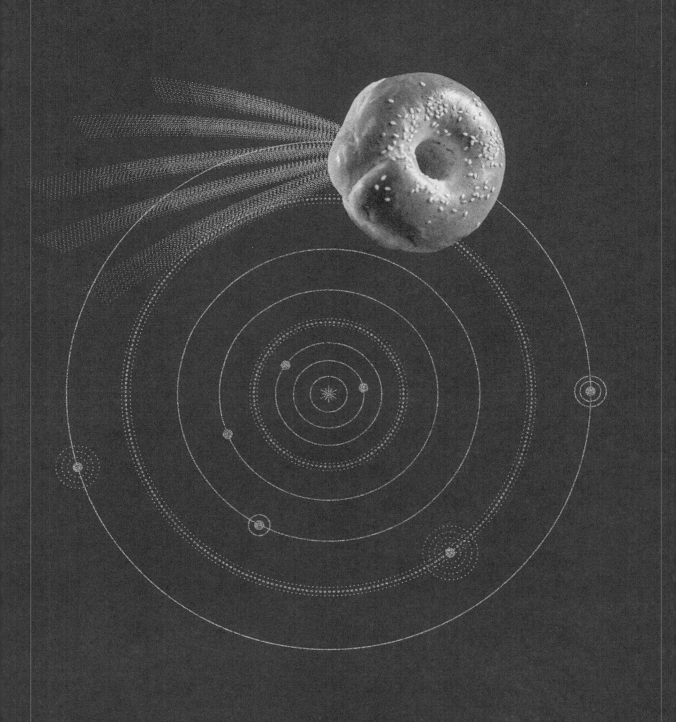

DOM PÉRIGNON'S FIRST POP

Much as it is hard to fathom life before the internet, it is hard for the wine industry to remember a time before Dom Pérignon, fine wine's greatest marketing success. Dom Pérignon started out as a special release by the large Champagne house Moët & Chandon. Moët created the label in honor of a seventeenth-century monk and cellarmaster named Dom Pierre Pérignon, who was formative in the creation of Champagne. He was the first to use red grapes to make a white wine (now a commonplace practice), and legend has it, he accidentally discovered that carbonation could happen naturally in the bottle, giving still wine the bubbles for which Champagne is known. But this special release's contents were identical to Moët's mass-produced product. It was just aged for slightly longer before release to add complexity, then sold in a nostalgic-looking bottle with a different label. This lipstick-on-a-pig (albeit a very delicious pig) tactic remained in place until 1943, when Dom Pérignon became its own special blend.

Moët & Chandon bottlings between 1921 and 1943 are of a much higher quality than the Moët littered throughout the world today. Moët, now one of the largest producers of the stuff, prioritizes putting Champagne into the most hands possible, rather than being an exemplar of quality taste. But its Dom Pérignon label is, thankfully, the exception. Despite being a trope for glitz and glamour, Dom Pérignon is still high-quality Champagne worthy of both celebrations and collecting.

Mary Sherman Morgan, the inventor of the jet fuel that carried the first American satellite into orbit, is born. (She wants to name her invention "Bagel," since the propellant it uses is liquid oxygen, or LOX, but the US Army fails to share her sense of humor.)

French bartender Fernand Petiot allegedly invents the Bloody Mary while working at the New York Bar in Paris. A favorite haunt of Ernest Hemingway, Coco Chanel, and Jean-Paul Sartre, the bar is later renamed Harry's after another of its bartenders.

The phrase "cold turkey," in reference to quitting an addiction, appears in print for the first time. It is most likely an evolution of the expression "to talk turkey," which means to tell someone something honestly.

1921

GONE WITH THE GAUDICHOTS

ONE OF THE BENEFITS OF COLLECTING WINE IS THE OPPORTUNITY TO follow a specific bottling's flavors from vintage to vintage. The practice is not unlike following your favorite sports team season after season. The age of the vines is like the quality of the roster; the varying weather is the injuries and suspensions; and, of course, the winemaker's hand that brings it all together is much like the coach or manager. And in the same way a newly minted billionaire might eye a team with an outgoing owner, wineries look for acquisitions.

In 1929, one of the wine world's greatest trades was in the works when Domaine de la Romanée-Conti (DRC) angled to acquire a large parcel of the La Tâche vineyard from the Comtesse Liger-Belair. The Liger-Belair family had owned the legendary vineyard for more than a hundred years by then. It overlapped the DRC vineyard of Les Gaudichots in the Burgundian town of Vosne-Romanée. Needless to say, the Liger-Belair family was not thrilled at the idea of other wineries using the La Tâche label for wines from vineyards outside their proper La Tâche section. Fights, court cases, and drama ensued surrounding the use of names that later would be declared by law. So in 1929, DRC released Gaudichots from the vineyard that is now only sold as La Tâche. Later, DRC successfully petitioned the local governance to call their entire vineyard holdings La Tâche. While their acquisition of La Tâche benefited the quality of their wines, no La Tâche wine has a greater allure than the never-to-be-made-again Gaudichots bottling of 1929.

The Roaring Twenties come to an end with Black Thursday, the first of many enormous stock market crashes. One silver lining is that the Great Depression is credited with hastening the end of Prohibition, as the government can no longer justify the expense of enforcing the unpopular law—plus, everyone really needs a drink.

Toy salesman Edwin S. Lowe comes across the game Beano at a carnival near Atlanta. Intrigued, he brings it back to New York. One of his friends is so excited when she wins that she accidentally shouts, "Bingo!" The name sticks.

Bell Telephone Labs gives one of the earliest demonstrations of color television with the broadcast of images of the American flag, a man eating some watermelon, and a pineapple, all on a screen the size of a postage stamp.

1929

PRIDE AND PORT

DESPITE ITS GEOGRAPHIC ORIGINS AND NAME, PORT IS MORE OF AN English wine than a Portuguese one—the English invented it out of necessity during a blockade with France in the 1600s. The grapes were harvested and the wines produced in Portugal, but it was sold by English shippers. The Brits went gaga for the sweet and powerfully viscous liquid that turned from a cherrylike syrup into something subtly herbal and a bit like black tea if given enough time. Many of the names we recognize on the dark, stumpy bottles today are those of the original Brits: Warre, Graham, Dow, Taylor, and others. The drink even embodies the class distinctions of English society—from the workhorse ruby port to bottles that are practically royal (single quinta vintage port).

Different styles of port are determined by how long the producer ages the wines, as well as where the grapes come from. It's a common, if quantity-over-quality-oriented, practice in Portugal's Douro Valley for port producers to buy grapes rather than grow their own. Ruby port is aged for the shortest period of time and can be a blend of grapes from almost anywhere in Portugal. It's not very sophisticated. Meanwhile, single quinta vintage port must be from a specific vineyard harvested in a specific year. Declaring a vintage for port only happens around three times a decade. This is the good stuff.

If one port were the equivalent of, say, Queen Elizabeth II at the height of her reign, it would be 1931 Quinta do Noval Nacional. This is the port of all ports. Phylloxera destroyed nearly all rootstock in Europe (see page 24), yet a small plot on Quinta do Noval's property survived unblemished. It's from those old, native vines that this iconic port is made. Its name, Nacional, is a patriotic nod to those resilient, now century-old vines.

NYC's Empire State Building officially opens after 410 days of construction. It holds the title of world's tallest building until the World Trade Center's north tower surpasses it in 1970.

President Herbert Hoover signs a bill making "The Star-Spangled Banner" the national anthem of the United States. The melody originally belonged to an English drinking song.

Ellery J. Chun, the son of Chinese immigrants, graduates from college and returns to Honolulu to manage his family's dry goods store. Noting the colorful clothing in fashion at the time, he begins selling shirts cut from flashy kimono cloth, and trademarks the name "aloha shirt" in 1936.

1931

SWEET AS SUGAR: DESSERT WINE

During the Age of Exploration, as the maritime powers prepared for their transatlantic voyages, one pressing question was on every sailor's mind: *What are we going to drink?* Roiling seas and equatorial heat are a perfect recipe for turning wine to vinegar—especially in the absence of proper storage and refrigeration (see page 20)—so if the libations were to last on those monthslong journeys, they would need to be very special indeed.

Enter fortified wines. A catchall term, it refers to wine with both high alcohol and high sugar content. (Past a certain alcohol by volume percentage, yeast can't survive, and any sugar that might have otherwise been turned into alcohol remains as is.) Think: port and sherry, among others. The residual sugar and additional alcohol added following the first fermentation act as a preservative, pulling water out of organisms that might contaminate the wine, desiccating invaders by force. This is the same reason honey has been used as a preservative since ancient times. Sherry successfully voyaged to the Americas with Columbus in 1492, and Magellan took a stash on his journey, making it the first wine to travel around the world—if any of it was left by the end. Not only did these sweet wines not deteriorate with age, many actually got better over time. Madeira, for instance, made in its namesake Portuguese colony off the coast of Morocco, became tastier and more velvety as it sloshed its way to the American colonies. The wine's cooked-grape method makes it virtually indestructible, and today, you can still find a good bottle from the 1700s with relative ease.

Sweet wines enjoyed a high status with land-bound Europeans, too, as sugar was an expensive luxury commodity at the time. The ultimate in aristocratic treats was Tokaji, a sweet wine made in Hungary from grapes left on the vine in hopes that a fungus commonly known as noble rot would take hold. During the rotting process, the fungus sucks water out of the grapes, turning them into raisins, concentrating their flavor and adding notes of ginger and honey. It only happens in lucky years, when the conditions are exactly right. The intense sweetness of the resulting Tokaji made it "the king of wines, and the wine of kings," per the Sun King himself, Louis XIV.

Over the ensuing centuries, though, these after-dinner drinks, which used to be the most important in the world, became about as fashionable as the name Norma. (Sorry, Grandma.) Wine storage techniques improved, and transporting and aging non-sugary wines became possible. Poor imitations in other countries hurt the style's reputation, too, and the definition of luxury also shifted. As palates moved on from heavy, creamy food to lighter, spicier cuisine, beverage tastes inevitably followed. In a recent attempt to revive sweet wine's status, desperate Sauternes producers paired with Perrier to market it at trendy Parisian bars, but by and large, their golden age is a thing of the past.

PROHIBITIVELY RICHE

THE PERIOD FOLLOWING WORLD WAR I WAS A GOOD ONE FOR WINE, marking the beginning of fine wine production outside of port, Champagne, and Bordeaux. One place, however, that most definitely didn't flourish was the United States, which was stuck under the thumb of Prohibition from 1920 to 1933. During this period, the nation's vineyards survived by selling sacramental wines to churches, DIY wine kits (only to men), and, of course, bootleg juice to anyone risk tolerant enough to partake. When Prohibition ended at the tail end of 1933, the few California wineries that survived—namely Inglenook, Charles Krug, Beaulieu Vineyard, and Beringer Vineyards—were not what they once had been. Their first post-Prohibition vintage, 1934, was merely okay, but it was better than no drink at all. At least for the first time in fourteen years, California winemakers had nothing in front of them but opportunity. Well, opportunity and a massive economic recession to deal with.

Meanwhile, over in France, Domaine de la Romanée-Conti released one of the best wines of Burgundy of all time: the 1934 Richebourg Vieux Cépages. As a whole, DRC's catalog of wines is like Quincy Jones's discography—unmatched in its breadth of accolades and revered by everyone who's even vaguely familiar with the stuff. But their 1934 Richebourg Vieux Cépages, of which only about one hundred bottles were produced, is peerless in the world of wine. While the Richebourg vineyard is generally overshadowed by DRC's more famous Romanée-Conti and La Tâche vineyards, especially now that it's been replanted, its old, pre-phylloxera vines were one of a kind. The original rootstock yielded a wine of deeper color, flavor, and nuance than the new roots that exist today. In 1934, the winery bottled the grapes from these old vines separately to create this unicorn of a vintage.

Amid a wave of dictators rising to power around the world, Adolf Hitler declares himself Führer.

The *Daily Mail* publishes a photo of the Loch Ness Monster as "proof" of its existence.

The Apollo Theater in Harlem reopens after closing during a campaign against burlesque. It hosts its first amateur night contest.

1934

THAT HURT:
THE IMPACT OF PROHIBITION

As illegally tipsy as we might have been throughout Prohibition, by the time it ended, it had had a profound effect on America's wine industry: we'd forgotten how to drink wine.

Prior to Prohibition, our drinking culture rivaled Europe's. We imbibed at every meal, and factory work even had a designated time for some grog. And the wine industry, at least on the West Coast, had been flourishing. Spanish missionaries, needing communion wine, had taken some vines from the Old World and planted them around the Americas as they moved. Hardy and drought-resistant, the mission grape, as it came to be known, was ideal for the American Southwest.

But all that changed with the passage of the Volstead Act, which specified the Eighteenth Amendment's rules. The "capital T" teetotalers had won out and the United States became a fully dry country. Panicked, winemakers desperately tried to figure out how to survive. Some tried to convert their wine grapes to table grapes or jam; some ripped up their vineyards and replanted them with avocado and walnuts; others just closed. In Missouri, which had been the nation's second-largest wine-producing state, nearly all the wineries shut down. The ones that did survive thanks to loopholes—Beringer made dehydrated grape bricks (exactly what it sounds like) for those DIY wine kits, Georges de Latour found its religious side, and a few took advantage of the allowance for prescription alcohol—didn't make it out unscathed, either. Millions of acres of native and mission vines had been ripped up in favor of alicante bouschet, a grape with red pulp whose juice is so dark it's almost purple-black. It was perfect for grape bricks—you could make double the amount of wine with the same volume of grapes by diluting with water and spiking with sugar. The problem was that it was double the amount of shitty wine.

So by the time everyone could take a legal drink again, no one wanted to touch wine. Why have gross alcoholic juice when rum and bourbon were available? When Americans *did* reach for wine, they only wanted dizzyingly sweet stuff (looking at you, Mateus and Lancers). Not until soldiers were introduced to the European way of life during World War II did the rest of us remember there was something more out there. As a whole, Americans didn't develop a taste for dry red wine until the late 1960s, which was fine, because it took decades for winemakers to undo the damage of alicante and recultivate good varietals.

BETTER THAN COOKING WINE

1937 WAS THE LAST GREAT EUROPEAN VINTAGE BEFORE THE TWENTI-eth century's most significant shift in wine, and arguably society: World War II. The following year suffered from poor weather, and fighting had begun before most grapes were harvested in 1939. In Burgundy, in particular, 1937 was an exceptional year. The weather was ideal, and it was clear upon release that the firmly structured wines had the potential to age for many decades.

Burgundy in the 1930s was replete with winemakers who would become superstars. Legends-to-be like Georges Roumier, René Engel, Henri Gouges, and the Marquis d'Angerville were at the early stages of their careers. These young guns broke with the common practice of selling wine, good or bad, at a low price and in high volume. If their grapes weren't of the very best quality, or if things went awry during fermentation, they simply wouldn't sell the wine. At the time, this type of care, attention to detail, and financial sacrifice were exceedingly rare.

Michel Lafarge was one of those discerning young winemakers. Still inexperienced back in 1926, he had failed miserably despite the year's excellent harvest. Rather than sell the wine and put the reputation of his family's winery at risk, Lafarge took every bottle and used it to cook a mountain of coq au vin. In 1934, Michel finally made a wine that he thought was worthy of the family name, and three years later, his 1937 was extraordinary. It would go down as one of the domaine's greatest-ever bottlings. Though Lafarge died in 1940, his legacy for rustic, classically rooted wines lives on. Lafarge wines didn't chase trends back then, nor do they now.

The modern age, in all its overprocessed glory, blasts through this year, with DuPont patenting nylon and Spam making its debut.

Pablo Picasso paints *Guernica*, bringing global awareness to the Spanish Civil War.

***Snow White*—Disney's first** animated feature—premieres on the same day Dr. Seuss publishes his first book: December 21, 1937.

1937

CALIFORNIA'S FIRST STAR

AFTER SURVIVING PROHIBITION AND JUST BEFORE THE START OF World War II, Georges de Latour, the owner of Beaulieu Vineyard in Napa Valley, traveled to France. His goal was simple: rebound from the devastation of Prohibition by making better wine. He sought the help of French-trained Russian refugee André Tchelistcheff, who, after Georges's visit, relocated to Napa Valley in 1938. Upon his arrival, Tchelistcheff tasted a bottle of Latour's "private reserve," which was typically only for family consumption. Tchelistcheff's first bit of advice: make more of whatever that was.

Latour released the first vintage of private reserve for commercial consumption in 1940 under Tchelistcheff's direction and winemaking. This vintage—and the updated techniques used to produce it, including controlling temperature during fermentation—represented a new benchmark for Napa, and for American wine in general. Tchelistcheff had permanently changed the American wine industry. From that point on, California wine was on an upward trajectory—though Beaulieu's quality dropped off rapidly after it was acquired by a conglomerate in 1969. It was later reacquired and sold multiple times, and as a result, the only period of note for the producer's wines is that vaunted stretch from 1940 to 1968.

A year into World War II, German bombers begin the Blitz, a campaign of aerial attacks on British towns.

Oglethorpe University, just outside Atlanta, Georgia, seals off a 2,000-square-foot time capsule. Scheduled to be opened in 8113, the "Crypt of Civilization" includes books, a toy Greyhound bus, and voice recordings of Benito Mussolini, Popeye the Sailor Man, and a champion hog caller. No wine is included, but a wineglass is.

"Bésame Mucho," written by Mexican composer Consuelo Velázquez, is recorded for the first time. It will go on to become one of the most covered Spanish songs of all time.

1940

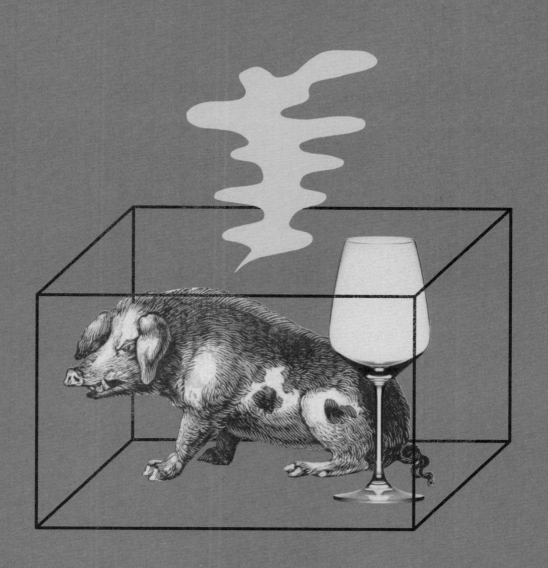

PART II

GENERATION OLD SCHOOL
(POSTWAR TO 1989)

Without question, World War II was an enormous tragedy. Following it, the sentiment among winemakers was that during those six years, progress had been made in their field. For one, farmers gained technological advances like gasoline- and electric-powered machinery, as well as pesticides and chemical fertilizers, which brought some relief to farming's challenges. Global trade routes were streamlined and an abundance of artisanal goods from around the world followed, including wine from smaller producers, thanks to the rise of groundbreaking American importers like Robert Chadderdon, Becky Wasserman, Kermit Lynch, and Leonardo LoCascio. This expanded import market, combined with a rise in curiosity from consumers about the flavors of different places, led to an interest in wine as both a technical product and a luxury commodity. People began drinking beyond just their local wine, and the concept of "dining out" took hold as well, meaning more nice wine was on more tables.

After the war, most winemakers continued to be both farmers and vintners. This generation became the first to successfully implement organic and biodynamic farming techniques while, for the most part, maintaining the wine-making techniques of their predecessors. Wineries from many different regions began to garner new respect as they experimented with these novel farming techniques, paying closer attention to the impact they were making on their land. In regions like Italy, Burgundy, and California, the first celebrity winemakers emerged.

The wine from this time is all the more precious now because it can never again be replicated. These spectacular postwar winemakers didn't have to contend with the greatest challenge winemaking would face in the twentieth century: climate change.

ONE IN SIX HUNDRED

LIKE THE SUN COMING OUT AFTER A STORM, 1945—THE FIRST POSTWAR vintage—marks one of the greatest ever in France. And metaphors aside, the sun really did shine in abundance in 1945, especially compared to the rainy, cloudy conditions in both 1944 and 1946.

During this era, simply put, the top vintages were the ones that experienced the warmest weather. (Remember, this was before global warming, when warm weather was still moderate and always a good thing.) A sun-kissed season gifted the grapes with enough sugar to turn from sour to lush, and a hot year produced more of those sweet grapes, which led to more wine, which generated more money, which gave people a reason to celebrate.

While many wines were excellent this year, one garnered a reputation greater than any other: 1945 Domaine de la Romanée-Conti from the Romanée-Conti vineyard. Including it in a book about the most memorable wines in history is a bit like saying Aretha Franklin and the Beatles are important to the history of music. "Respect" and "I Want to Hold Your Hand" will always be playing, and this wine will always have the admiration of every connoisseur (even if most, including this book's author, have never tasted it).

The grapes that produced this vintage were from those rare and miraculous survivors: vines still growing on their original, pre-phylloxera French roots. But by this time, these elderly vines bore very little fruit. Only six hundred bottles were produced, whereas in normal years, ten times that number come to market. The vintage is spectacular, of course, but its scarcity is also part of what makes it so valuable. After 1945, because of their incredibly low yields, the vines were torn up and replanted with a different type of rootstock. The next vintage this vineyard produced was not until 1952.

Considering the ideal weather in 1945, it shouldn't come as a surprise that Romanée-Conti wasn't the only standout wine. In Bordeaux, for example, the harvest was celebrated for grapes with rich flavors and the vintage was hailed for its potential to age for a long time (see page 62). The predictions weren't wrong. A pristine 1945 Bordeaux from a top chateau will still be fresh and full of life today. These legendary wines manage to have a both silky and chewy texture, with the classic aromas of tobacco, spice drawer, and bitter chocolate.

In fact, 1945 marks the beginning of a long period of the region's greatest hits. Many argue that it was the best year for Mouton Rothschild, Haut-Brion, and Petrus, but was 1945 really better than '47, '49, '53, or '59? Hard to say. You won't find any misses among those iconic postwar vintages in Bordeaux.

Penicillin, the miracle mold juice that was a game changer on the battlefield, is finally produced in great enough quantities that Americans can buy it at the corner pharmacy.

After the war ends, the US government imports eighty-eight German scientists to help with their rocket program. Let's just say background checks weren't a priority.

Grand Rapids, Michigan, becomes the first US city to fluoridate its drinking water. The cavity rate drops by 60 percent.

1945

AGE IS JUST A NUMBER: OLD WINE

Well-aged wine is like a cup of tea. Herby, even spicy in some cases. These earthy, floral, leather, cigar-like notes—including acquired tastes like hay, stone, and mushroom—are known as a wine's tertiary flavors and are revealed over time as the wine's primary (fruit, jam) and secondary (oak, butter) flavors subside. A beautiful old Burgundy, for instance, that had been berrylike in its youth, may be floral and savory at peak maturity.

Luckily, wine doesn't hit its peak only to fall off the cliff the next day. Wine reaches perfection—maximum complexity, ideal mouthfeel, pleasingly soft tannins, and balanced acidity—in a gentle arc and, thankfully, decays away from it in a similar slow fade. A principle called Coates' Law of Maturity states that a wine will remain at its ideal for the same amount of time that it took to get there. Finding a particular vintage's peak window is an art rather than a science, though, and where that window begins very much depends on personal preference. For example, the Brits have historically preferred their Champagne on the older side—less fizzy, more biscuity—while the French prefer theirs to be like Leonardo DiCaprio's girlfriends: young and exuberant.

(It is also worth noting that some wines can taste pretty bad in the time between their youthful fruitiness and peak maturity. This is called its "dumb phase." Everyone has an awkward period at some point.)

Past peak maturity, wine begins deteriorating. While too many tannins in a young wine can make it astringent—causing that puckery drying sensation—losing too many tannins from excessive aging results in a wine without structure. Wine that's too old tastes lifeless and dull. The flavor of poorly aged and spoiled wine can run the gamut from Worcestershire sauce to vinegar to wet dog.

WRONG BANK, RIGHT WINE

AS A VINTAGE, 1947 HAS SO MUCH NOTORIETY THAT A RESTAURANT with three Michelin stars in Courchevel—France's equivalent to Aspen—uses the year as its name and inspiration. If that's not enough, restaurant Le 1947 is in a five-star hotel named after what's considered the top bottle of that year: Cheval Blanc. It should nearly go without saying, then, that 1947 Cheval Blanc is the epitome of fancy.

Cheval Blanc didn't always conjure fur coats, freshly ironed sheets, and fine dining. Despite some successful vintages in the 1920s, the name didn't mean much until this year. The winery is located in the town of Saint-Émilion, which, in conventionalists' eyes, was on the wrong side of the tracks—or at least the wrong side of Bordeaux's two rivers. Producers like Lafite, Latour, Margaux, and Mouton, all of which grow mostly cabernet sauvignon, are Left Bank legends, positioned south of the Garonne River. But Saint-Émilion, north of the Dordogne River, is considered Right Bank, where the main grapes are merlot and cabernet franc. These varieties produce less robust wines than those made with cabernet sauvignon, a fact that, combined with the Right Bank's relative shortage of marquee producers, has led many to think of it as the inferior bank.

In 1947, one thing even the snobbiest Left Bank enthusiasts couldn't argue with was the weather. The warmth gave Cheval Blanc's grapes a sweetness that had rarely been achieved before. The result of those elevated sugar levels was a polished, muscular wine that has aged beautifully for the better part of a century. Now, though, the 1947 vintage is famous not because of its taste, but simply because it's long been recognized as the greatest. As the saying goes, the rich get richer.

These 1947 Right Bank Bordeaux wines were blessed with the same weather as Cheval Blanc, and while exceptional in flavor, have not enjoyed the same global hype:

- Château Ausone
- Château Latour à Pomerol
- Clos l'Église-Clinet
- Vieux Château Certan

After ruling India for nearly one hundred years, the British finally shove off.

Rancher W. W. Brazel reports that a mysterious "flying disc" crashed onto his property. The next day, a public information officer confirms that the army successfully recovered the flying disc—then swiftly retracts the statement.

Chuck Yeager becomes the first person to officially break the sound barrier. He wasn't really allowed to tell people because, you know, state secrets. This is the year the Cold War begins, after all.

1947

BIGGER ISN'T ALWAYS BETTER

DOMAINE GEORGES ROUMIER WAS STARTED AS A SIDE HUSTLE, WHICH, for reference, is the equivalent of Mozart moonlighting as a wedding DJ for extra cash. Georges Roumier is considered one of Burgundy's greatest winemakers of the twentieth century. But before he built up a reputation of his own, he was an employee at the larger Domaine Comte Georges de Vogüé from the 1920s to 1955. During his tenure there, one wine—the phenomenally rich and concentrated 1949 vintage from Vogüé's best vineyard, Musigny—skyrocketed and solidified Roumier's reputation as the master of Musigny. Having gained the locals' respect as a star, Roumier's name held clout, which was saying something. It was still early days for winemakers and landowners selling wine under their own names and labels, and the smaller-scale, more farm-to-table approach of doing so was a financial risk that most could not tolerate. But when Roumier set out on his own, the reputation of his perfect 1949 Grand Cru of Musigny under the Vogüé label was enough to support wines under his own label for generations to come.

Of all the vineyards in all of Burgundy, the Grand Cru of Musigny exemplifies the delicate and subtle flavors of pinot noir more than any other. The red wine vineyard is easily in the top five in the whole region. But unlike some of its peers—La Tâche and Romanée-Conti, to name a couple—Musigny has ten different owners. Today, Vogüé still owns almost 70 percent of Musigny, while Roumier owns about 1 percent. Roumier's slice is only large enough to produce about 350 bottles per year. While Vogüé is synonymous with Musigny thanks to its large stake, Roumier is the source of its best wines and is synonymous with the best stuff.

Most of the great vintages of this period are considered such because of their power and richness. But not all great wine must be big wine, and a vintage like 1949 in Burgundy and Bordeaux proves that. By all measures, the year was warm, but the September rains caused the sugar levels in grapes to drop and, in turn, produce wines with lower alcohol levels. Château Mouton Rothschild 1949, a wine some consider the best Mouton of the century, was only 10.7% ABV. An average ABV for any wine is around 12.5% and as a point of comparison, the recent highly acclaimed release of 2016 Mouton clocked in at at least 13.5%. Normally, high alcohol means rich wine, which means high aging potential, which means high perceived value. But the finesse and exceptional evolution of the 1949 vintage proves that wrong.

The World War II–era rationing of sweets ends in Britain on April 24, 1949, but leads to such a sugar rush that rationing is reintroduced four months later.

Astronomer Fred Hoyle coins the term "big bang" on a BBC radio broadcast. Ironically, he was making fun of the theory, and he spent the rest of his life fighting against the idea.

In Berlin, Herta Heuwer invents currywurst thanks to some curry powder from British soldiers stationed in the city.

1949

AUSTRALIA'S DEBUT ALBUM

PRIOR TO 1951, NOT MUCH ABOUT AUSTRALIAN WINE IS WORTH DIS-
cussing. To be fair, the same is true for almost all the world's wine
regions outside of France. That all changed in 1950 when Max Schubert,
Penfolds's winemaker, traveled to Europe and was inspired to make his
own wine that could age and be cellared. Upon returning to Australia, he
employed versions of winemaking techniques and vineyard practices that
he had observed at Bordeaux estates like Latour, Lafite, and Margaux.

As is the case in the United States, wines in Australia are made
largely from French grapes. Down under, they call syrah by another
name, shiraz, really for no reason other than to try to differentiate it
from the grapes grown in France. Syrah always makes wine that is dark
and full of flavor, but in the dry heat of South Australia, it's particularly
rich and nearly black in color.

Thanks to his newfound knowledge, the year after his life-changing—
and industry-changing—trip, Schubert bottled the first vintage of Australia's most prized wine, Grange. He used fully ripe, heavily extracted
shiraz from a blend of vineyards, and Grange set the benchmark for dark,
concentrated Australian red wine. Big, weighty shiraz continues to be the
signature of Australian reds to this day.

In Mexico City, Carl Djerassi, Luis
Miramontes, and George Rosenkranz
develop synthetic progesterone.
Originally intended to prevent
miscarriage, it later becomes the key
ingredient in birth control pills.

Henrietta Lacks dies of cancer in
Baltimore, Maryland. Without her
consent or her family's knowledge,
her cells are cultivated for research.
Some estimate that if all the cells
ever grown from her line were
weighed on a scale, they would
measure 50 million metric tons.

The United Nations, formed in 1945,
moves out of Lake Success to its
permanent headquarters on the east
side of Manhattan.

1951

ON A MISSION

LIKE SOME CHILD STARS, PLENTY OF WINES START OUT FULL OF PROMise and hype, only to disappoint with age. But there are also bottles initially considered "pretty good" that eventually blossom into something extraordinary. The wine that takes home the title of Greatest Glow Up might be the 1955 La Mission Haut-Brion. Slowly, impressively, and quietly, it has overtaken its peers. As critic Robert Parker once said, "Even allowing for the greatness of Haut-Brion and Mouton Rothschild, the 1955 La Mission is the wine of the vintage."

So why no fireworks upon the wine's release? The lack of celebration certainly had nothing to do with its flavor or structure. Simply put, La Mission Haut-Brion didn't come from Médoc, the better-known region of Bordeaux. Rather, it hailed from Graves. If the Médoc is Shakespeare, Graves is Beckett. Or if the Médoc is Adele, Graves is Grimes. The point is, Graves just didn't have the cachet. What's become clear in the intervening decades is what the region did have—a potential for exceptional wines that has only been realized by the two Haut-Brion houses: La Mission Haut-Brion and its neighbor Château Haut-Brion (see page 131).

Fifteen-year-old Claudette Colvin refuses to give up her seat to a white passenger on a bus in Montgomery, Alabama, nine months before Rosa Parks does the same. Claudette is hauled off the bus and arrested.

Milkshake mixer salesman Ray Kroc opens the first McDonald's franchise a year after he noticed and looked into a huge order from one of his restaurant clients in Southern California, which was run by the McDonald brothers.

Elvis Presley, who begins the year playing high school auditoriums in Texas and Mississippi, is, by the end of it, the hottest new star in the music business.

1955

BIG BARTOLO ENERGY

WHILE FINE WINE PRODUCTION IN FRANCE BOUNCED BACK QUICKLY after World War II, it would be well over a decade before Italian wine-makers made the switch from producing table wine for local restaurants to focusing on quality and nuance. Italians still viewed their vineyards as pieces of land that needed to be maximized to pay the bills, and most of the wine produced was just for personal consumption. Even for now premier regions like Barolo, winemaking wasn't about garnering international accolades or marketing to collectors. As a result, most old Barolo from the 1950s and earlier was not properly stored, leaving us with a lot of spoiled bottles and little reference for how these wines might have aged. The oldest and most consistent top-quality vintage that can still be found is 1958—and one of the year's best efforts was Cantina Mascarello.

Bottles of 1958 Cantina Mascarello—now labeled as "Bartolo Mascarello"—were sold to local brokers in all shapes and sizes. Back then, glass was reused, and large demijohns—now used for terrariums and cheesy floral décor—were vital in distributing wine around town. A local restaurant would buy one, decant the wine into smaller bottles, and then return the demijohn to the winery for a refill, kind of like you might do with a growler from a local brewery. The options were the regular-size 750-milliliter bottles we know today, as well as the now illegal 1.9-liter format directly from the winery. These bottiglione, or big bottles, now extinct due to sizing standardizations, were sold for decades. They featured a variety of different labels, but the wine inside was always the same—and, remarkably, quite good. Some were adorned with "Cannubi," since that was the most famous vineyard of the time and a small part of the Bartolo blend. Some said "Riserva" to suggest a more limited release. And others just listed "Barolo" alongside the winery's name. It is hard not to find the irony in the family using whatever marketing terms it could to move its wares now that this coveted wine is nearly impossible to find.

Today, the winery is run by Maria Teresa Mascarello, whose father, Bartolo, continued the family legacy from the golden years of Barolo in the 1960s to today. Although Bartolo never saw himself as a blue-chip star, others did, and most of his work is now collected, hoarded, and enjoyed in worlds much more rarified than the local restaurants it was originally intended for.

The peace symbol, designed by Gerald Holtom, makes its first public appearance at an anti-nuclear war march in London. The downward lines are the flag semaphore signal for the letter N, while the central vertical one is the letter D: N(uclear) D(isarmament).

In Japan, Momofuku Ando invents the world's first instant noodles.

***Tennis for Two*, considered the** world's first video game, is released to entertain bored visitors at Brookhaven National Laboratory.

1958

AGING LIKE BALTHAZAR: BOTTLE SIZES

Maybe you've only seen magnums in the windows of wine stores, in restaurants dripping with candle wax, or in the hands of Formula One champions, but rest assured, big bottles of wine exist for more than just show.

A standard 750-milliliter wine bottle equates to about five individual glasses. Large-format bottles hold anywhere from two to forty times that amount. A magnum is the introductory big boy, at two times the size. Get any larger than that, and you'll find that most of them are named after Old Testament kings— Jeroboam (6 bottles), Salmanazar (12 bottles), Nebuchadnezzar (20 bottles). While you'd likely serve a Nebuchadnezzar just to prove that your budget is also of biblical proportions, wine in large bottles does, in fact, age more slowly.

To understand why, we've got to dip into some science: the evolution of flavor inside any bottle happens when oxygen slowly changes the wine's chemical composition. Remember, no matter the bottle's size or shape, there's always a little bit of air left in the neck of the bottle, and only the wine at the surface interacts with it. The smaller the ratio of wine at the surface compared to the overall amount of wine in the bottle, the less quickly the bottle ages. Imagine two swimming pools with the same dimensions, but one is *way* deeper than the other. While you can dive much farther in one of the pools, the number of spots from which you can come up for air is the same in both. The deeper pool is basically a magnum. The neck is the same size, but the volume of wine is twice as great, which means the effect of the same amount of oxygen is diluted over a greater amount of wine. No matter the year or the cellar, any larger-format bottles will taste fresher and more youthful. Conversely, half bottles shouldn't be cellared at all, and many producers have moved away from bottling 375 milliliters for this reason.

THE ROYAL FAMILY OF WINE

COMPARING ROSÉ FROM DOM PÉRIGNON TO WHISPERING ANGEL IS THE equivalent of judging *Citizen Kane* against *Space Jam 2*. One is an all-time classic, while the other is consumable but perhaps objectively bad. In 1959, the first release of Champagne's best rosé was produced in tiny quantities. Legend has it that the only bottles to have left the winery were for the Shah of Iran to commemorate the 2,500th anniversary of the Persian Empire. If any rosé is worthy of any such celebration—and happens to pair well with Persian food—it was this one. Because it was made from pinot noir and pinot meunier, two red grapes, then blended with chardonnay, a white grape, the finished wine was full, deep, and age-worthy. A bottle of 1959 could work for the 2,600th anniversary, too.

Alongside this greatest rosé of all time is also one of the best vintages of the great wines from Rousseau in Burgundy. In 1959, Armand Rousseau, who founded Gevrey-Chambertin's Domaine Armand Rousseau, died tragically in a car accident, leaving the responsibility of one of the century's top vintages to his mourning son Charles. Thankfully, the odds were in Charles's favor. The weather started the vintage right, and similar to the rosé blend of Dom Pérignon, making great wine from pinot noir also seemed effortless this year. Like Jean-Luc Godard and Kylian Mbappé, the 1959 Rousseau, from the premier cru vineyard of Clos Saint-Jacques, is an expression of France's best. Although it isn't technically ranked at the highest level of Burgundy's quality hierarchy, Clos Saint-Jacques produces one of the most complex and distinct wines in Burgundy. Gevrey-Chambertin is wrongly stereotyped as being a big and robust version of pinot noir from Burgundy. There's no clearer argument against the notion that Gevrey only makes earthy and dense wines than the Clos Saint-Jacques bottlings from Rousseau. It's a wine of roses and pure class.

While Champagne and Burgundy are in the royal family of wine, in 1959 another star emerged—but not from noble blood: Lebanon. Yes, wine is made in Lebanon, and at least one wine here is worth mentioning (and drinking). That is Chateau Musar, and it's thanks to Serge Hochar, who took control of his father's winery in 1959. Serge learned to make wine in Bordeaux, and he applied those experiences by planting Bordeaux grapes back home in the Bekaa Valley. The result is a shocking wine—shocking in that its color is pale, its flavors are deep, and its age-ability is on par with any top Bordeaux or Burgundy.

Motown Records, the label that would define an entire generation of sound with the Supremes, the Jackson 5, and Stevie Wonder, is founded by Berry Gordy Jr. in Detroit, Michigan.

Fidel Castro, sworn in as premier of Cuba, calls the job "the toughest test of my life."

Alaska becomes the forty-ninth US state. America had purchased the territory from Russia ninety-two years earlier. An unpopular decision at the time, the land was ridiculed as "Andrew Johnson's Polar Bear Garden."

1959

BETTER DAYS

ANOTHER YEAR IN WHICH THE QUALITY OF WINE WAS HIGH JUST ABOUT everywhere: 1961. Bordeaux—check. Burgundy—yup. Champagne—you know it. In Barolo, in addition to being a great vintage, 1961 was also the beginning of a new chapter for two proud yet humble winemakers. For the first time, both Prunotto and Vietti chose to put the name of their vineyards—Bussia and Rocche, respectively—on their Barolo labels.

In 1961, though Barolo had long been a source of wine, most consumers didn't yet know about the region, or its fragrant grape, nebbiolo, so they certainly wouldn't have recognized the name of any small single vineyards or their unique characteristics. Naming specific places on these wine labels was a sign of Barolo's postwar move toward quality. Over the ensuing decades, listing prized vineyard sites on labels became the norm, and the wine market came to recognize Barolo as Italy's premier region. The 1961 vintage and the generation's pioneering winemakers—including Beppe Colla (Prunotto), Alfredo Currado (Vietti), Teobaldo Cappellano (Cappellano), and Angelo Gaja (Gaja)—are considered the foundation that today's success was built upon.

Turning an eye to France, we can't talk about 1961 without mentioning the syrah-based wine La Chapelle. It comes from the Hermitage region on the Rhône River, which is the world's greatest source of this peppery and floral red grape. Unlike the aforementioned Barolos, La Chapelle is not a single-vineyard wine, but rather a proprietary name that the winery Paul Jaboulet Aîné uses only for its top wines. The 1961 is their magnum opus. Any collector who has tasted it counts this wine in their top ten. But the sad truth is that over the span of a century, fewer than a dozen outstanding vintages of Paul Jaboulet's Hermitage La Chapelle were produced. After 1991, they changed their style, and the new one lacks all of its previous personality. Those who have tasted good bottles of pre-1991 Jaboulet versus post-1991 note its transformation from one of France's most authentic and prized producers to one of its biggest disappointments. But the 1961 is so magnificent that it redeems the failures of today. In fact, its legend may be what's still keeping the lights on.

Ten months after arriving in New York City, a twenty-year-old Bob Dylan makes his Carnegie Hall debut. Tickets are $2.00. Only fifty-three are sold.

Southern writer Harper Lee becomes the first woman in nearly twenty years to win the Pulitzer Prize for Fiction with her debut novel, *To Kill a Mockingbird*.

The Antarctic Treaty comes into effect, safeguarding the continent as a scientific preserve and banning all military activity. Because we don't have enough polar stuff to worry about, it will be up for review in 2048.

1961

BACK IN THE SSR

BRUNO GIACOSA IS OFTEN CELEBRATED AS A "TRADITIONALIST" OF Barolo and Barbaresco. This label is given to those who make wine less about sweet and oaky flavors and more about the pure and unadulterated potential of the grapes. Conversely, the "modernist" is criticized for using more controls during fermentation, excessive oak aging, and other techniques that shift the wines toward uniformity. It's a bit like comparing your grandma's pasta sauce to a tornado-shaped spaghetti pile adorned with the essence of basil on a pretentious chef's tasting menu.

But the moniker is deceiving. Giacosa was the most innovative winemaker in the region—and he made wines that epitomized the elegant and floral style that is now so sought after. Giacosa crafted exceptional wines from 1961 to 2008, and his most important wine came in 1964: the first vintage of Santo Stefano Riserva. Santo Stefano is a single vineyard in the town of Barbaresco, a region that neighbors Barolo and rivals its quality. These two places are in a sort of Yankees-versus-Mets matchup (if the Mets were also good). Giacosa only made the wine in nine other years: '71, '74, '78, '82, '85, '88, '89, '90, and '98. He hit a home run every time, but the 1964 stands out because it was Giacosa's first-ever single-vineyard bottling, helping affirm a trend that would put both Barolo and Barbaresco on the world wine map.

The five Fendi sisters open their flagship store in Rome's historic city center. A year later they hire a young, relatively unknown designer: Karl Lagerfeld.

Though the US surgeon general declared a causal link between smoking and lung cancer in 1957, it's not until a bombshell government report is published this year that the average American becomes worried about it.

A month after becoming the heavyweight champion of the world, Cassius Clay reintroduces himself as Muhammad Ali.

1964

MONDAVI SLAPS

IF THERE IS ONE WINEMAKER WHO BOTH HATERS AND OBSESSIVES OF American wine would agree is most important, it's Robert Mondavi. Mondavi's wine journey began when his family bought Charles Krug, a winery that had survived Prohibition and amassed significant land holdings in Napa Valley. The Mondavis weren't connoisseurs; rather, they were Italian immigrants with an entrepreneurial skill set that had led them to fortune, not once, but a few times over. After a trip to Europe, the eldest son, Robert, came back as the family snob, insisting that quality, not bulk, would be the future of Napa wine. Although he was neither the first nor the only person to believe in the potential of California wine, he certainly proved to be the most daring. After opening his own winery in 1966—the first built in the US since Prohibition—success followed, and with it, the rise of California wine from jug to jewel. Up until the 1990s, Mondavi made California cabernet in the old style, meaning Bordeaux-like. Rather than the big flavors of chocolate syrup and cherry pie you'll find today, they were lower in alcohol, with herbal and tobacco flavors, as well as exceptional ageability. Mondavi shifted hands in 2004 when the corporation Constellation Brands acquired it for several hundred million dollars. At that point, the daring move to make better wine paid off in a literal sense, but we all lost a source of great wine from America.

Mondavi was the first of many second-generation Californians who forged their own wine path rather than simply continue their family's legacy. Duncan Meyers and Nathan Roberts (Arnot-Roberts), Tegan Passalacqua (Turley), Morgan Twain-Peterson (Bedrock), and Diana Snowden Seysses (Snowden) are all industry-born Californians who have gone on to make a name for themselves outside of their family businesses.

In recognition of her contribution to hemlines creeping up throughout the decade, Mary Quant—the fashion designer credited with the invention of the miniskirt—is awarded the Order of the British Empire medal. Quant believed that high hemlines represented "life and tremendous opportunity."

Terrified by the burgeoning psychedelic era, the US government makes LSD illegal—though of course that ban didn't apply to its own clandestine experiments (I see you, MK-Ultra).

The Black Panthers write their Ten-Point Program, calling for jobs, education, adequate housing, and an end to police brutality.

1966

THAT GAJA GUY

In 1961, when Angelo Gaja started working at his family's winery, situated in the northern part of Italy, he quickly developed a reputation as one of the most passionate figures in Italian wine. Ambition is not always a good look in towns that pride themselves on tradition and respect, but Angelo's goal was to make the best wine, and he let that be known to all. Within a few years, Angelo had taken his family's winery to the next level—and along the way, he managed to elevate the entire Italian wine industry.

The first wine that showed Gaja's talent was the 1967 Sori San Lorenzo. Sori San Lorenzo is made from a single vineyard in Barbaresco, the lesser-known neighbor of Barolo. The inaugural release was adorned with a zigzagging red-and-chrome label, making it one of the first instances of an Italian wine aiming to create a brand recognizable visually rather than just by good taste. The wine was celebrated as spectacular back then, and still is today. It's got an ethereal harmony from the balance of its intensely floral and fruity aromas and the tart and bitter taste of its grape, nebbiolo—especially as those sharper flavors meld into gentler, easier-to-drink ones that only become more apparent over time. Its plaudits gave Angelo the confidence to travel the world selling his wine for use not only as casual Italian table fare, but also as an alternative to the country's greatest bottles from places like Barolo and Tuscany. It was a wine on the level of France's greatest, too.

Gaja's success continued until the late 1980s. The winery is still in business today, but its era of greatness ended in 1990, when Angelo introduced French barrels to Barbaresco and planted chardonnay and cabernet vineyards among the traditional nebbiolo. Introducing French grapes and techniques in the region was and is still looked down upon by most, and these wines do not get the same respect that the classic Barbaresco bottlings do.

One Hundred Years of Solitude is published by Colombian novelist Gabriel García Márquez.

Welsh scientist Tom Parry Jones invents the electronic Breathalyzer, and the UK introduces the country's first legally enforced blood alcohol limit. Jones's device unfortunately does not share the name of the first-ever roadside breath-testing device, introduced in the 1930s: the drunkometer.

The Outer Space Treaty, an international agreement that includes a ban on the placement of weapons of mass destruction on the moon or elsewhere in space, takes effect.

1967

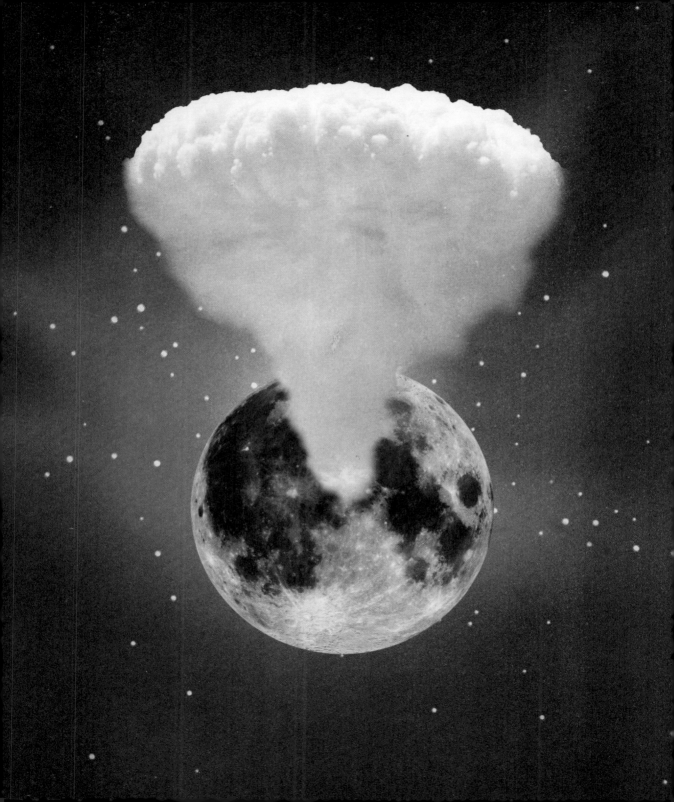

SOMETHING SUPER'S HAPPENING HERE

IF YOU'RE A FRANCOPHILE BORN IN 1968, THEN YOU'RE OUT OF LUCK for a birth-year bottle. If you're an Italian-obsessive, however, then you're sitting pretty. While 1968 was a wet disaster in Bordeaux and Burgundy, conditions were ideal in two parts of Italy, resulting in some of the country's best wines of the century.

The first was Bolgheri, a remote and rugged area of Tuscany that, to this day, contains little more than a spattering of big villas, vineyards, and olive groves. At the time, this was a place to rest and relax rather than grow grapes. No part of the region was famous enough for consumers to recognize by name, so the wines were labeled "vino da tavola," or table wine. This was the lowest rung on Italy's quality hierarchy according to the governing body that had just been formed and still exists today (see page 108). It was here that the Incisa della Rocchetta family decided to plant two Bordeaux varieties—cabernet sauvignon and cabernet franc. The Rocchetta family has produced two popes, and at one point, they could ride a horse from Florence to Rome without ever leaving their property. In 1968, Marchese Mario Incisa della Rocchetta—who, as far as family legacy goes, had some big shoes to fill—decided to begin selling the wine he had previously been making for his own consumption. That wine has since become perhaps the most well-known red in all of Italy: Sassicaia. The family's decision to plant here and Mario's decision to sell here were good ones. Since 1968, Sassicaia has grown in scale, but it has never diminished in quality.

South of Bolgheri, wine is made in the region of Taurasi, which owes its reputation to the Mastroberardino family's 1968 mastery of a dark and powerful grape called aglianico. The greatest wines they ever made are without a doubt from this year. In fact, this vintage showed so much potential that they decided to make single-vineyard bottlings, which had never been produced before, nor have they been since. The individual wines were from the three main towns of their vineyard holdings: Montemarano, Pian d'Angelo, and Castelfranci. Mastroberardino still exists, but unlike Sassicaia, its annual reunion tour is a continual disappointment. Although the winery had some hits before 1968 and a few immediately following, these bottles are generally considered one-offs from what was once among Italy's most promising wineries.

It was a year filled with violence and tumult: the assassinations of Martin Luther King Jr. and Robert F. Kennedy, race riots, the Prague Spring, and the Mỹ Lai massacre, to name a few.

Roy Jacuzzi invents the first commercial whirlpool bath. His great-uncle Candido Jacuzzi had designed its precursor for his son Ken after the child was diagnosed with systemic juvenile rheumatoid arthritis and told he wouldn't live beyond age three. Hydrotherapy helped him live past age seventy.

Meanwhile, orbiting the moon, the crew of Apollo 8 become the first humans to experience the "overview effect"—a sense of overwhelming awe and oneness with the planet that comes from seeing Earth as a fragile ball in space.

1968

UNDER THE TUSCAN SUN: SUPER TUSCANS

Like almost all wine-producing regions, Tuscany has strict laws governing which grapes can be used when the name of that region is stated on the label. For example, a bottle that says Brunello di Montalcino must be 100 percent sangiovese, while a Vino Nobile di Montepulciano need only be 70 percent. Throughout the 1960s and '70s, several winemakers aligned in thinking that they could make great wine outside of those restrictions. The result of these efforts— the nonclassified wines that came to be known as the "Super Tuscans"— represent both their best efforts and, legally, their poorest.

For most consumers, a Super Tuscan denotes a big, powerful wine. Many of today's better-known Super Tuscans are blends of Bordeaux varieties full of structure, tannins, and body, like cabernet sauvignon and merlot. Most of these wines get high point ratings year over year, including the imprimatur of the ultimate in bold wines: 100-point scores (see page 134). The confusing thing is that Super Tuscan also refers to wines of drastically different styles. For example, a group of the top winemakers in Chianti Classico use 100 percent sangiovese, a light and earthy grape. Up until recently,

it was illegal for a Chianti Classico to use just this grape, so these delicate wines were also classified as Super Tuscans, despite vastly different flavors from the better-known, and quite intense, Tignanello (sangiovese + cabernet sauvignon + cabernet franc) and Sassicaia (cabernet sauvignon + cabernet franc). In short, Super Tuscan is a not-so-helpful term— the only way to have an idea of what one tastes like is by knowing which grapes are in the bottle—but many great wines have come from this spirit of rebellion.

Light and earthy Super Tuscans (some of the best wines in the whole region):

- Fèlsina Fontalloro
- Fontodi Flaccianello
- Isole e Olena Cepparello
- Montevertine Le Pergole Torte

Big and rich Super Tuscans (more like Bordeaux):

- Antinori Tignanello
- Masseto
- Ornellaia
- Sassicaia
- Solaia

NEW GIGS GONE RIGHT

IN THE 1960S, WHILE SOME PEOPLE JOINED COMMUNES, MADE TIE-DYED T-shirts, and celebrated being in their youthful, idealistic stage of life, Jacques Seysses bought vineyards in Burgundy, acquiring a defunct winery for its land rather than for its equipment, which was in near shambles. Born the son of a well-to-do biscuit manufacturer in Paris, Jacques had the good fortune to be able to choose his own path in life. (At the time, becoming a winemaker was not a job most parents would be excited for their child to pursue, much like parents today might not be bragging about their kid dreaming of becoming an Instagram influencer.) Jacques's first vintage in 1968 was so terrible that it's best left unmentioned—but it's a good thing he wasn't easily dissuaded. He got his act together quickly, combining traditional techniques with a focus on making a delicate style of red Burgundy, and his land held up its end of the deal. In 1969, with garden-size slices of vineyards in Clos de la Roche, Clos Saint-Denis, Gevrey-Chambertin Aux Combottes, Echézeaux, and Bonnes-Mares, Jacques made some of the greatest wines in this generally exceptional vintage.

At the same time, but on the other side of the winemaking world, a guy named Paul Draper was hired at Ridge Vineyards, nestled in the cool Santa Cruz Mountains of Northern California. These mountains are California's coldest growing area for cabernet sauvignon, leading to delicate and earthy flavors reminiscent of great Bordeaux. Paul, a recent Stanford graduate, had gone to Chile to make wine in a nineteenth-century manner: no irrigation, no temperature controls—just naturally made wine with the intention of quality over commerce. Impressed, the owners of Ridge Vineyards—a group of Stanford Research Institute scientists who purchased the remote property to escape the oncoming wave of technology—invited Paul to return home to California. You can see how their interests aligned.

In 1969, Draper released his first vintage at Ridge: the bottling of Monte Bello, a single vineyard on the crest of the Santa Cruz Mountains. Paul Draper's hands-off approach allowed the hyper-local wine to ring true of its place, and this 1968 Monte Bello bottling—a light, old-school style of cabernet, reflecting that mountain climate—won Paul and his team international praise. Ridge became one of the first California wineries to emulate the European practice of making wine from a single site year after year at a time when much of California wine was a blend of different vineyards across the region. Still today, that winery and its vineyards and facilities are of a different era. Ridge just has good mojo.

Walking really hits its stride this year: Neil Armstrong takes his small step on the moon while the Beatles take theirs on the cover of *Abbey Road*.

Yellowstone National Park officials try to force local grizzly bears to return to a wild diet. More than two hundred of them are unable to give up junk food and are killed because of the danger they pose to visitors.

Plane hijackings go sky-high with nearly ninety planes diverted, most of them to Cuba. The phenomenon is so common that *TIME* magazine runs an article titled "What to Do When the Hijacker Comes," which suggests passengers bring a bathing suit to enjoy their overnight stay.

1969

IT NEEDS MORE TIME

BAROLO IS A PLACE THAT FEELS RUSTIC AT HEART. THE TOWN, FILLED with old houses and covered in an eerie layer of fog, has only a couple of traffic lights. Life moves slowly there, and the wines do, too. Plenty of Barolo wines are approachable when they're relatively young, but Mascarello isn't one of them. It isn't an exaggeration to say that the 1970 Mascarello—dense, elegantly bitter, and tannic like a black tea—may not even be ready to drink today.

Many of the most seasoned drinkers of Italian wine have said that 1970 Giuseppe Mascarello Barolo Monprivato is one of the best wines the boot-shaped country has ever produced, kicking the much-better-known names and higher-rated vintages to the side. The Mascarello family had been blending the grapes from the Monprivato plot into their Barolos for years, but in the ripe, balanced, and generally excellent 1970 vintage, they decided to release it as their first single-vineyard specialty bottling. It was the perfect choice. Their wines from the 1950s and '60s are still in good shape, but the 1970 Monprivato is the hallmark of the winery's history. It is as firm, rustic, and old-school as any in the Mascarello portfolio, but it's also got complexity and elegance on top of this intensity.

Monprivato is still bottled today as the family-run establishment's top wine, and while Mascarello has had highs and lows since that winner in 1970, their wines remain noteworthy for their ability to age. That said, while longevity is a stamp of quality, it's infuriating when any wine is considered too young to drink even after its fifty-year anniversary.

The first Earth Day is celebrated on April 22, marking the birth of the modern environmental movement.

To commemorate the one-year anniversary of the Stonewall Riots, Chicago and San Francisco host the first gay pride parades on June 27. Los Angeles and New York quickly follow suit in the same year.

On December 21, Elvis Presley meets in secret with President Nixon. He offers to help with the war on drugs in exchange for a badge from the Bureau of Narcotics and Dangerous Drugs. Nixon agrees, and the King surprises the president by hugging him.

1970

A TIME FOR WHITE WINE

THE 1971 VINTAGE RANKS AS ONE OF THE CENTURY'S BEST IN BUR-
gundy, Barolo, Champagne, and the Rhône Valley. It's an exceptional vintage for reds, but if there were a podium of the year's best bottles, the
white wines would sweep. The weather was consistent and neither too
hot nor too cold, gifting the wines lots of acidity, a natural preservative of
freshness. Unfortunately, aging white wines wasn't a common practice at
the time, so most bottles were consumed early and, sadly, are now extinct.

That drink-now mentality is still common, but it doesn't need to be.
Indeed, some white wines are eminently cellar-worthy. To start, Laville
Haut-Brion is one of the few estates in Bordeaux to make only dry white
wine, and they are certainly the greatest of their kind. Like almost any
white Bordeaux, Laville Haut-Brion is a blend of sémillon and sauvignon
blanc. Most sauvignon blanc around the world is aged in stainless steel.
It's mass-produced and tastes like grapefruit juice and jalapeño. But
Laville Haut-Brion ages theirs in oak barrels, leading to a regal white that
tastes like honey, guava, and flowers. The 1971 vintage has such a precise
structure and freshness that those flavors have persisted over time.

La Coulée de Serrant, a single vineyard in the Loire Valley of France
where only chenin blanc (a grape known for its potential to age) is planted,
is another safe bet. The best versions taste like salt, apples, and lemon.
The Joly family bought the vineyard in 1962, and for many collectors,
Coulée de Serrant's best era is the 1970s and early 1980s, before Nicolas Joly, an innovative natural producer, joined the family business and
moved the winery away from its traditional practices. Their 1971 is a
perfect example of a pure, classically made wine, and is emblematic of
the fact that natural isn't automatically better.

If chenin blanc gets old gracefully, then riesling built from the 1971
vintage ages like the pyramids. And while Trimbach's Rieslings are the
crème de la crème in France's Alsace region (see page 117), Egon Müller
is das beste in Germany. Riesling is a grape that can do it all, and so
can maverick Egon Müller. Working in the Saar, a remote region of Germany, he makes wines that range from dry and citrusy to thick and sweet
as syrup. Some 1971 Müller wines from the Scharzhof vineyard range
are slightly sweet, while others have sugar levels higher than jelly. The
sugar helps preserve these wines, even as the perception of its sweetness
dissipates over time. The 1971 Kabinett—a less sweet designation on
riesling's scale—now tastes like a totally dry wine. At the other extreme,
Trockenbeerenauslese is the sweetest on that spectrum and can only be
made in select vintages. The grapes need to be of such good quality in
their youth that they can stay on the vines for an extended period, eventually leading them to dehydrate, which concentrates their flavors, sugar,
and acidity.

Buying oysters year-round is legal
again in New York. Governor
Nelson Rockefeller repeals the law
prohibiting sales between May and
August, which had been set in 1912
when there was little refrigeration to
keep shellfish from spoiling in the
summer months.

Eleven doctors and two journalists
who believe that people's right to
medical intervention transcends
state lines found Doctors Without
Borders on December 22.

Shirley Chisholm, the first Black
woman to serve in the House
of Representatives, enters the
Democratic primaries for the 1972
presidential election.

1971

CHARDONNAY SAUCE

LIKE A NEW CAR, THE CARIBBEAN SEA BREEZE, OR A NEW YORK CITY sewer, California chardonnay has a specific scent and flavor. Today, the production of California chardonnay is abundant and a bit dreary (depending on who you ask), but in the 1970s it still had an air of distinction and elegance. In fact, it had such an aura that even the French gave it some credit.

In 1976, France held a blind wine tasting called the Judgment of Paris. Napa Valley's Chateau Montelena entered its 1973 chardonnay, and the wine famously took home the grand prize, shocking its French competitors. How significant was the difference? Not very, but the American wine industry has drawn a seemingly unending amount of marketing material from this tale. In truth, 1973 in Burgundy as a whole was good but not stellar, while thousands of miles away in California, the vintage was praised consistently. That's not to discredit the wines from Chateau Montelena. They were good—best described (begrudgingly) as French-like, meaning less oily and more tart than other California chardonnay.

But the wine that took second place in the Judgment of Paris is more indispensable to the world of wine overall: Domaine Roulot. Roulot has consistently produced some of the world's best chardonnay, beginning in the 1970s and continuing to this day. Roulot is based in Burgundy in the town of Meursault, where the style is all about subtlety and saltiness, diametrically opposed to the rich and creamy chardonnay prevalent in California. For what it's worth, if Roulot had entered a wine from their Meursault-Perrières vineyard rather than Charmes, they would have undoubtedly taken first prize.

California isn't all bad. If you want your chardonnay to taste like wine—rather than like buttered popcorn—try these producers:

- Ceritas
- Hirsch
- Lioco
- Matthiasson
- Sandhi Wines
- Tyler Winery

1973

A BAD YEAR'S BEST BOTTLE

WHILE 1974 ISN'T A SOUGHT-AFTER VINTAGE FROM THE COMMONLY COLlected regions, one bottle from that year is so distinct and delicious that it sits on the short list of the twentieth century's best wines. Even skeptics of the wine world's overly poetic descriptions would agree on how to describe this legend: Heitz Cellar Martha's Vineyard bottling tastes like mint chocolate chip ice cream.

Joe Heitz started making wine in Napa Valley in the late 1950s alongside California's new generation of winemakers, including the pioneering Robert Mondavi. He originally acquired a small vineyard planted with the obscure Italian grape grignolino, but it wasn't this pale, rosé-like wine that brought Heitz fame. It was a vineyard called Martha's Vineyard, planted with cabernet sauvignon and owned by friends of Joe and his wife, Alice, that would put Heitz on fine wine's international stage. The first vintage from this vineyard was 1965, but the still-young vines yielded wines without much complexity. With another decade under its belt, the organically farmed Martha's Vineyard produced grapes with unmatched nuance. Old vines grown in soil surrounded by an abundance of eucalyptus trees make this one of America's most distinctive vineyards. Although Heitz might have fallen out of fashion, its quality has remained consistent. Today, under the supervision of Master Sommelier Carlton McCoy, it's having a second lap of success.

The first surviving set of sextuplets is born in South Africa on January 11. Their father is awarded full custody during a divorce fifteen years later. In one parent-teacher conference day, he has to see twenty-six teachers.

On August 9, Nixon becomes the only US president in history to resign.

Humanity sends an interstellar radio message from Puerto Rico's Arecibo Observatory. It includes the numbers one through ten, a representation of the DNA double helix, and a stick figure drawing of a person. ET doesn't seem impressed— or at least doesn't respond.

1974

FROM ROOTS TO RICHES

WHEN COMPARING ANY WINE ACROSS MANY VINTAGES, YOU'LL OFTEN find that its first release is its best. Celebrating an early win is easy, and frankly, comparing sequential years isn't fair, given the lack of control a winemaker has on nature's impact. However, when you look at the body of work of Henri Jayer, one of the most important figures in postwar Burgundy, the early, the late, and everything in between is outstanding. Jayer, who passed away in 2006, is remembered as the flawless hand behind season after season of one of the most consequential wines in French history: Cros Parantoux.

Jayer began making wine under his own label in the 1950s and continued to do so with great success until his final vintage in 2001. Although he produced bottlings from Burgundy's most renowned vineyards like Echézeaux and Richebourg, his celebrity was cemented with the garden-size vineyard Cros Parantoux. Cros Parantoux is high on a hill—a position that doesn't usually earn the same respect as vineyards lower on the slope—and following World War II, the vineyard had gone fallow. Jerusalem artichokes occupied Cros Parantoux's rows of vines. Jayer saw the vineyard's potential when others didn't; after all, he knew that its neighbors were some of the most expensive and sought-after vineyards in the world. Jayer quite literally chipped away at stones, replanted little bits of the vineyard, and purchased additional plots from other landowners in order to eventually produce pinot noir grapes of the highest quality. He waited until the vines aged and the grapes met his requirements before finally releasing Cros Parantoux as a standalone bottling in 1978.

While Cros Parantoux's fantastic first vintage is labeled "1978," legend has it that the Henri Jayer Vosne-Romanée 1976 is actually Cros Parantoux. Even though 1976 is not a superhero year for Burgundy, this wine from the hand of Jayer has stood the test of time. Its delicate and soft flavors have morphed glacially into an earthy yet still fruit-driven taste—a success only the magic of Jayer could have produced.

Patty Hearst, who popularized the phenomenon Stockholm syndrome when she seemed to sympathize with her Symbionese Liberation Army captors, is found guilty of bank robbery.

Red M&M's, dyed with Red No. 40, disappear during a red food panic after a study links another artificial red dye with cancer. They remain absent for eleven years until Paul Hethmon, a college student in Tennessee, starts the Society for the Restoration and Preservation of Red M&M's as a joke, but one that catches on. When Mars reintroduces the candy in 1987, they send Hethmon fifty pounds in celebration.

An expedition team led by paleontologist Mary Leakey finds animal prints preserved in volcanic ash in Laetoli, Tanzania. They later discover that the site is also home to 3.6-million-year-old human footprints, proving that these early humans were bipedal, but likely had very short legs.

1976

THE CHIANTI CLASSIC

A DARING ENDEAVOR WOULD BE TO ALTER THE WINEMAKING TRADItion in a region as steeped in history as Chianti. Chianti is the world's best-known region for table wine—wine that's meant to be enjoyed alongside food in the company of loved ones rather than exalted. In America, drinking Chianti in the 1970s was common, but it certainly wasn't cool; Italian wine was mostly served in a wicker basket—always the cheapest bottle on a restaurant's list. Most Chianti at the time blended sangiovese with French varieties such as cabernet and merlot to give color and softness to the tart and herbaceous Tuscan native. There's nothing wrong with the sentiment of a simple bottle of Chianti, but a handful of producers aspired for more than Nonna's approval. Their mission: produce higher-quality wines using the region's sangiovese grape exclusively.

Le Pergole Torte was one of the first—and absolutely one of the best—of these new sangiovese-only Chiantis, beginning with its initial release in 1977 from the Montevertine winery. Pergole Torte helped show the world that both sangiovese as a variety and Chianti as a region deserved to be taken seriously. It would be another twenty years before the American market treated Italian wine like it already treated bottles from France—that's to say, as a sign of luxury. But Pergole Torte was always one of Italy's stars.

New York's now famed Studio 54 opens with exactly the fever-dream party of your wildest imagination. Think: Dolly Parton and Cher on the dance floor and a line outside so long even Frank Sinatra gives up and goes home.

Stephen King publishes *The Shining*, *Rocky* wins best picture, and *Star Wars: Episode IV—A New Hope* premieres.

The year that gives us Cookie Crisp cereal is also, thankfully, the year scientists develop synthetic insulin.

1977

THE PERFECT FLIGHT

THE USUAL PROGRESSION OF WINE AT DINNER IS TO START WITH A crisp glass of white, work your way through progressively bolder flavors, and end with a big red. The Platonic ideal of that wine flight in a single vintage is 1978—specifically Raveneau Chablis to start and Giacomo Conterno Monfortino for the finale.

Today, Chablis—an area of France that grows only chardonnay—is considered one of the premier white wine regions of the world, but that was not the case in 1978. Back then, the grape was known to make wines dry and crisp, or, more bluntly, simple and cheap. The Raveneau family was one of the first in the region to take inspiration from winemakers in nearby Burgundy. They aged their Chablis in oak barrels rather than the more common steel tanks, giving the wines Champagne-like savory flavors while still maintaining Chablis's classic sharp edge of freshness. These more costly methods didn't yet have a market to support their added expense, so Raveneau did the work out of passion rather than practicality. The result in 1978 was some of their best ever—and this vintage is still fresh today.

As we move through the meal, only a few wines could possibly follow and complement the powerful flavor of this Raveneau, and none better than Giacomo Conterno Monfortino. For decades, the Conterno family made wine exclusively from purchased grapes, until 1974 when they bought a hayfield called Cascina Francia. (It was a deal that almost didn't happen. In the final hours of negotiating this purchase, the seller tried to increase the price. Giovanni Conterno was irate, but his wife insisted he get the deal done and not to return home until he did. The strong negotiator—who had his priorities straight—made it back in time for dinner.) After a few years, the vineyard yielded grapes good enough for the already-regal Conterno name. And then, in 1978, the estate leveled up from all-star to legend when Conterno began releasing two bottlings from the vineyard: Barolo Cascina Francia and—the winery's top bottling—Monfortino. Like all wine with "Barolo" on its label, both releases were made with 100 percent nebbiolo. Compared to Cascina Francia, Monfortino was a more powerful wine with greater aging potential. While earlier releases of Monfortino had been made from grapes purchased across a variety of vineyards in the region, 1978 was the first vintage that was Conterno wine from seed to serving—and it was great.

On January 16, NASA names a new class of astronauts, the first in nearly a decade. The group includes Black, Asian, and female astronauts for the first time.

The world's first "test tube baby" is born in England on July 25.

Plastic bottles—lightweight, resealable, recyclable, and unbreakable—seem like a fine idea. Coca-Cola introduces the world to the two-liter PET plastic bottle, and it's a sensation.

1978

TWO PIERRES, ONE MONTRACHET

PIERRE RAMONET HAD BEEN MAKING WINE AT HIS EPONYMOUS WINERY in Chassagne-Montrachet since before the war. But in 1978, he was able to acquire the undisputed champion of white wine vineyards, Le Montrachet, which abutted his own. (Montrachet's legend is such that a New York City restaurant co-opted its name and became the city's first spot to obsess over Burgundy.) While 1978 is not considered a bad wine by any measure, the most knowledgeable collectors know that Pierre's second vintage of Montrachet, the 1979, was France's—and therefore the world's—best bottle of chardonnay.

Ramonet wasn't the only Pierre making Montrachet at that time. Pierre Morey's family had only a small collection of vineyard holdings, but they had agreements with other landowners, like the respected Lafon family, to expand their capacity and release more wine under their namesake label. Using grapes farmed by others, they would bottle Montrachet. Like Ramonet, Pierre Morey is a white winemaker, and like Ramonet, he's one of the century's best. Morey would go on to run Domaine Leflaive for the next twenty years, and his releases in the late 1970s and '80s were exceptional—epitomized by the all-time-great 1979. In cooler vintages like 1979, the sharp flavors of chardonnay play against the rich texture that the powerful Montrachet vineyard is known for, producing a balanced and distinctive wine with an aging potential of decades to come.

Disco fever persists, despite "Disco Demolition Night," a Major League Baseball publicity stunt staged between games during a Chicago White Sox doubleheader that quickly devolves into chaos. Thousands rush onto the field after an anti-disco shock jock explodes a crate filled with disco records, sending up shards of burning vinyl and leaving a hole in the outfield.

On July 1, the first Walkman— designed because Sony's cofounder wanted to listen to music on long flights—goes on sale in Japan.

Judy Chicago's _The Dinner Party_, a milestone of feminist art, makes its worldwide debut at the San Francisco Museum of Modern Art.

1979

THE FOOD AND WINE POLICE: WINE LAWS

Although prescription drugs are the largest exports of both France and Italy, there's no doubt that their food and wine are the exports that inspire the most pride. In an effort to protect the quality of the often multi-millennia-old industries and public perception of certain regions, both countries (along with the larger European Union) have adopted a protected designation of origin (PDO) agreement whose laws oversee and protect the collective brand association that consumers have with the names of countless regions, such as Barolo, Burgundy, Parmigiano Reggiano, and Comté.

Each of these regions, or appellations, has a sort of instruction manual (and naturally, the more prestigious the appellation, the more exacting the guidance). For example, if you're lucky enough to possess vineyard land in Chianti, and you want to make and sell wine with the region's name on the label,

you must follow the guidelines of the Chianti PDO, which regulate everything from grape type to harvest volume levels to details as granular as minimum barrel aging requirements. That said, some producers ignore the regulations of their specific geographical region and accept the downgrade for their wines' failure to adhere to these regulations (see page 88). In other words, just as no one can stop you from painting a landscape, but you're not allowed to say you made a Monet, no one can stop you from planting a certain grape in your backyard, as long as you don't say you made a Montrachet.

Depending on the country, the governing laws have different names, which can usually be found on the label. In France, the laws are more detailed under the Appellation d'Origine Protégée (AOP) system. Single vineyards, only a few acres in size, have boundaries protecting their names, which cannot legally be used unless grapes of the appropriate variety and quantity harvested are registered and checked by the governing body. The idea is that the vineyard name is not owned by the individual winery, but rather by the collective region, so its general flavor and therefore its grapes must be consistent regardless of who makes the wine. If and when a winemaker wishes to experiment with nonpermissible grapes, the wine is simply called *vin de France* ("French wine"). If some fool wanted to plant cabernet sauvignon in the Romanée-Conti vineyard, for example, that wine would be a vin de France, not having earned or fulfilled the requirements for the name of the most regal vineyard of all. Italy's program is called the Denominazione di Origine Controllata (DOC). The even higher level of regional quality—and the one with the strictest regulations—is the Denominazione di Origine Controllata e Garantita (DOCG). Only 73 DOCG exist in the country; two of those are Brunello di Montalcino and Barbaresco, both of which allow the use of only one grape variety (sangiovese and nebbiolo, respectively) and require extensive aging. The United States has its own laws, called the American Viticulture Area (AVA) system. State laws exist as well—if you put "California" on a label, for instance, all the grapes used must come from California, whereas in other states, the requirement is only 85 percent.

While limiting, wine law is ultimately good. Without it, selling a fake would be pretty easy. Indeed, for a long time, producers in the United States used European regional names like Burgundy, Chablis, and port. In 2006, the EU and the US came to a trade agreement banning those names from further use outside Europe, meaning (thankfully) we will never again see a Missouri Moselle or California Chianti.

THE BIRTH OF BETTER BEAUJOLAIS

In the early 1980s, wine consumers still looked to Bordeaux, Champagne, and port as the "nice" wines, and quaffed bad wine by the can and box when they didn't care as much. But the good stuff was being made elsewhere—and no one seemed to care. Burgundy was producing great bottles, but they were not yet collectible; Barolo was in its heyday, but few people noticed. So when a few winemakers set out to improve the reputation of a region considered remote until the late 2010s, it was a daring leap worthy of at least a few fire hoops. Hello, Beaujolais.

Beaujolais sits between Burgundy and the Northern Rhône Valley, just outside France's gastronomic mecca, Lyon. That is to say, it should be a place where quality is respected inherently. Instead, it became an area for making red wine in the fastest and fruitiest way possible, fermenting it using industrial yeasts and other ingredients to convert the juice into alcohol ASAP. This style is called Beaujolais Nouveau, and it's the wine equivalent of a TV dinner.

The first to say "we can do better than this" was Marcel Lapierre, who, in 1981, became an extremely early adopter of organic farming. In addition to that practice, he allowed his wines to begin fermenting naturally, meaning through ambient air rather than heading straight to a chemistry lab—a process that is now considered a prerequisite for any high-quality wine. He was also among the first winemakers to question the excessive use of sulfur in wine.

Why did he change his methods in 1981?

"Because the wines I made didn't satisfy me, and the wines from elsewhere that I liked weren't made in the modern style," Lapierre told the quarterly magazine *The Art of Eating* in 2004. "I'm just making the wine of my father and grandfather," he said, "but I'm trying to make it a little better." And better they were. Lapierre's darker, more savory wines showed the world that Beaujolais could be more than just gulpable wine. Other producers in the region took note, and Beaujolais has been on an upward quality trajectory ever since.

New dietary guidelines, written in haste after President Reagan pushed through a budget that slashed children's nutrition funding, count ketchup as a vegetable in school lunch programs. After massive blowback, some in the administration claim it was an oversight, and Reagan withdraws the proposal.

The era of the home computer firmly arrives as IBM enters the personal computer market.

Mauritania becomes the last country in the world to abolish slavery.

1981

SULF-N-PEPA: SULFUR IN WINE

Sulfur dioxide, or SO_2, villainized for the past three decades as a headache-causer, is an important antioxidant with antimicrobial properties. While it is a natural by-product of fermentation, it's also been added to wines as a preservative for centuries. Sulfur stabilizes a wine and its flavors, helping to keep it fresh during transport (as it does in dried fruits and syrups). In wine, it can also mask problems or flaws. But in large quantities, it can alter the taste of a wine. Think of it as salting a steak: just the right amount makes it better, but too much is bad, and maybe even dangerous. While some of the best wines in history contain some additional sulfur, most winemakers today try to use as little as possible. To add none, however, is a daring proposition, unless the wine is consumed locally and kept at a consistent temperature.

AND THE WINNER IS . . .

ROBERT PARKER'S NEWSLETTER ABOUT THE 1982 VINTAGE IN BORdeaux is an OG piece of viral content. Parker, the same guy who created the point system, is said to have changed the wine market forever when he shouted from his desk in Baltimore that these were the wines of the century. In the States, wine transformed seemingly overnight into a mass luxury product, and so marked was the beginning of wine as a status symbol, with producers, regions, and vintages becoming signs of wealth and decadence. And the wine most synonymous with this hyped-up (sometimes overhyped) vintage is Château Mouton Rothschild.

On the list of great vintages from Mouton, a winery as revered as any in Bordeaux, the flavor of 1982 doesn't rank near the top, but its fame certainly does. Why is it so well known? The year was hot and yielded a big crop. The resulting wines had a power and concentration not seen in any vintage of the entire preceding decade. The shift and newness gave critics like the suddenly influential Parker something to talk about. It was a look-alike to 1947, which until then had been the vintage of the century for Bordeaux. The 1982 Mouton Rothschild was bold and impressive, and its flavors were accessible for new consumers—plainly good rather than overly complicated. But thanks to the hype machine initiated by Parker and fueled by a new wave of consumers, 1982 became—and remains—one of the most expensive Bordeaux vintages of the past half century.

While Mouton Rothschild always occupies more than its fair share of the spotlight, Bordeaux's wine of the year in the grand vintage of 1982 is Château Lafleur. Château Lafleur is across the river from the Left Bank, long perceived as the land of big wines, extravagance, and wealth. The Right Bank, on the other hand, is far more approachable in both price and volume. Compared to Mouton, Château Lafleur is a mom-and-pop-type operation. Their total volume is less than one-tenth of Mouton's, but in 1982, size didn't matter. The 1982 Lafleur—a blend of merlot and the sharp and savory cabernet franc grape—is what insiders consider Bordeaux's wine of the vintage.

The Look of a Label

Even today, 1982 Mouton turns heads when it lands on a table, and not just for its big, bold reputation. The baby blue label is almost as famous as the wine itself. Designed by John Huston, best known as the filmmaker behind *The Maltese Falcon*, the watercolor features a ram gracefully leaping between the sun and grapes. This high-art label tradition dates back to 1924 when Mouton adorned their bottles with a cubist design from Jean Carlu. Chagall, Miró, Picasso, Bacon, Dalí, Balthus, Koons, and Richter are all Louvre-worthy names whose work you'll find in cellars across the globe.

On July 2, Larry Walters, a truck driver whose poor eyesight kept him from becoming a pilot, attaches forty-three helium-filled weather balloons to his lawn chair and soars 16,000 feet above Long Beach, California. When he lands fourteen hours later, police promptly arrest him. As he is led away in handcuffs, Larry tells a reporter, "A man can't just sit around."

In the town of Adria in northeastern Italy, Arnaldo Cavallari invents ciabatta bread as Italy's response to the baguette's soaring popularity in France.

The movie *E.T.* is the biggest box-office hit for the next eleven years, while the video game *E.T.*, also released this year, becomes known as the worst video game ever made. Game maker Atari secretly buries thousands of cartridges in a landfill in New Mexico.

1982

WHEN BEING LATE IS A GOOD THING

ALSACE IS A REGION IN EASTERN FRANCE FAMOUS FOR FOIE GRAS, SAUsage, and kraut. Not much pairs well with these foods other than, well, the white wines of Alsace—especially those honey- and flower-flavored wines made from the riesling grape. Riesling is commonly thought of as cloyingly sweet, and it can be, but the large majority of it is free of excess sugar and tastes uber refreshing. The masters of making such wine are the Trimbach family and their single-vineyard Clos Sainte Hune.

Year after year, theirs is one of the world's best and most collected riesling-based wines, known for consistency and precision. However, in 1983, Trimbach pivoted to make a wine of equal pedigree but a different flavor. That year, for the first time, Trimbach made a bottling of Clos Sainte Hune from late-harvest grapes, a style known as vendange tardive. They had left a small part of the vineyard to ripen for an additional month, yielding more concentrated grapes, honeyed in flavor and color. Often when white grapes ripen for an extended period, the result is a sweet wine like Sauternes. This gives the wine better aging potential, as a little bit of sugar goes a long way in terms of preservation. That said, 1983 Clos Sainte Hune is certainly not a sweet wine, but it does offer a unique subtle sweetness, and it's considered one of the great white wines ever to have been made outside Burgundy. Trimbach has only released its flagship wine in this slightly sweet style one other time since, in 1989.

If Clos Sainte Hune prides itself on being sharp and crisp, wines from Pierre Overnoy are wild and round—that's to say, the two couldn't be more different, but they both stand out in 1983. Overnoy, who took over his family's estate in the Jura region of France in 1968, was an early pioneer of natural wine. Today, the Jura is home to some of the most remarkable white wines in the world. No name in the Jura is bigger than Overnoy's. His winemaking style is what is referred to as oxidative: not unlike an avocado turning brown after it's cut open, white wines can brown, too. Oxidation is usually considered a failure by winemakers, but in the Jura—and in particular in the region's *vin jaune*, or yellow wine— it is the intention. With exposure to oxygen, the flavors shift from citrus and fresh fruit to roasted nuts and chamomile tea. The taste is closer to sherry than to classic white wine. In 1983, Overnoy released a vin jaune that's still widely considered one of the best ever made. Similar to the vendange tardive from Trimbach, vin jaune is only made in years when the grapes can be harvested later, giving the wines bigger, more concentrated flavors.

The polymerase chain reaction (PCR), a term now forever associated with nasal swabs and hoarding toilet paper, is developed by biochemist Kary Mullis, who credits the innovation to his acid trips.

The Global Positioning System (GPS), originally designed for the American military, is declassified and made available publicly to prevent future tragedies after a Korean civilian airplane is shot down when it accidentally strays into Soviet airspace.

Stanislav Petrov, a Soviet military officer, single-handedly spares the world a nuclear war by correctly identifying a US missile launch alert as a false alarm.

1983

PINOT GOES WEST

PINOT NOIR'S ANCESTRAL HOME IS BURGUNDY, BUT THE GRAPE HAS found its way around the globe. You can find well-made pinot from Argentina to New Zealand, Germany to Ontario. Perhaps its most well-respected vacation home is on the West Coast of the United States, in California. While red Burgundy (or French pinot noir) is detested by committed California-only drinkers for being too tart and earthy—like Henri Gouges's wine, for example—even the most critically acclaimed California pinot is hated on by savvy European drinkers when it veers toward supple, fruity, and oaky—like the in-your-face style Kistler and Marcassin make in Sonoma. Some wines in the center achieve a little bit of both. They have the California strawberry and plum scent, with a crisp, gentle taste that's more French-like—but tense party lines between Burgundy lovers and pinot lovers are as reliable as the Yankees–Red Sox rivalry.

Truthfully, though, in California, most pinot winemakers strive for the Burgundian profile. They've adopted similar label designs and bottle shapes; they've hired famous Burgundy natives as consultants; and in their marketing copy, the first descriptor is usually (the very subtle) "Our goal is a Burgundian profile." Sometimes it's true, and sometimes it's just a sales pitch. One of the first to make this shift, around 1978, was Josh Jensen of Calera Wine Company. Then came Hirsch, Au Bon Climat, and the producer responsible for California's first-ever pinot to retail for $100, Williams Selyem, on the Sonoma Coast.

Burt Williams and Ed Selyem first called their winery Hacienda del Rio but changed it to Williams Selyem in 1984 after being sued by another Sonoma winery named Hacienda. They made some of America's best light red wine from 1984 until the winery was acquired by businessman John Dyson in 1998. The Williams Selyem wines of the mid-'80s to the late '90s are regarded nostalgically as the most Burgundy-like wines ever to come from California. During this time, climate change had not yet caused pinots to be awkwardly full-bodied and high in alcohol, so they still maintained the chemistry to stay savory and age gently over time. Much California pinot noir lacks a unique identity; it's just fruity and jammy. But the magic of Williams Selyem, which began in 1984 with wines that were far from this mass-produced norm, is one of a kind— albeit inspired by France.

Russian computer programmer Alexey Pajitnov builds the prototype of *Tetris* in two weeks. He can't stop playing it at work.

Alec Jeffreys, a British geneticist, realizes that small repetitions in people's DNA might be enough to distinguish one individual from another and proves himself right when he develops the first successful DNA fingerprints on September 10. The technique first cracks a criminal case in 1987.

Sitting several feet apart at a silk- covered table, British prime minister Margaret Thatcher and Chinese premier Zhao Ziyang agree that the UK will return Hong Kong to China in 1997.

1984

Today's best French-style pinot noir producers outside of France are:

- Bodega Chacra (Argentina)
- Domaine de la Côte (California)
- Dupuis Winery (California)
- Failla (California)
- Littorai Wines (California)
- Presqu'ile Winery (California)
- Rhys Vineyards (California)
- Tyler Winery (California)

NEXT TO NIKE: OREGON PINOT NOIR

A bit up the West Coast of the US in Oregon, pinot is every bit as famous. Here, specifically in the Willamette Valley, it's considered a local grape rather than an experimental endeavor. Perhaps you've heard Oregon and Burgundy have nearly identical climates. Oregon isn't Burgundy in the same way that Emily isn't Parisienne. But they're pretty close, both possessing an ideal environment for preserving the freshness of the grape. Some serious wines from the Willamette Valley are noteworthy examples not just of American wine, but of pinot noir overall. Top Oregon pinot noir producers include Antica Terra, Evening Land Vineyards, and Walter Scott.

I KNEW YOU WHEN

THE YEAR 1985 WAS ONE OF THOSE "IT WAS GREAT EVERYWHERE" KIND of vintages. The weather was warm and consistent, which was a welcome change from the year before—a European vintage generally skipped and/ or forgotten due to flood-like rains during the months of harvest. Zooming in on France's Rhône Valley and Burgundy, the good news is that in 1985 the wineries Guigal and Ponsot produced the best wines from their respective regions—Côte-Rôtie in the Rhône Valley, and the Clos de la Roche vineyard in Burgundy. Now for the bad news: these are some of the last-ever great vintages from those producers.

Guigal was on the short list of most sought-after syrah producers on the planet. They had been making high-quality wine for decades, including many notable triumphs in the 1960s and '70s. In 1985, they made the full trio of their "La La" bottlings: La Landonne, La Mouline, and La Turque—the latter of which they made for the first time that year. These bottles are well rated and collectible thanks to a lighter hand with oak, which allowed the subtleties of the syrah grape to shine through. Indeed, these wines are more comparable to Bordeaux than Burgundy, and like the Bordeaux from 1985, they are still improving with age. An old syrah from the pure style of 1980s Guigal tastes like lavender, freshly cracked black pepper, and the fanciest bacon you've ever eaten.

A two-hour drive north on the A6 from Côte-Rôtie, Domaine Ponsot has a history in Burgundy dating back to the late 1800s. However, like many others in Burgundy, the family name did not appear on the labels of their wines until the 1930s. Ponsot was considered remarkable but not truly A-list until Laurent Ponsot took charge of the winery in the early 1980s. Laurent is one of those figures about whom everyone has something to say, though not all of it is glowing. That said, all would agree that he's an independent thinker—which isn't always a good thing in the world of wine. Laurent's vintages, from his first in 1983 to his last in 2017 (when he announced he was leaving the family business "effective immediately") varied wildly depending on his whims and experiments. But in 1985, Laurent Ponsot didn't go as off script as in subsequent vintages, and he took advantage of old vines, ideal weather, and ripe grapes to make a wine that was concentrated, earthy, and decadent. The 1985 Clos de la Roche is the absolute apex of the Ponsot name. These wines are pure, precise, and fawned over, even if there isn't much fawning over Laurent today.

Scientists working for the British Antarctic Survey discover a hole in the ozone layer.

Long Island's Carmela Vitale changes the pizza takeout game when she receives the patent for a plastic "package saver," the mini table that prevents the box's cardboard lid from sinking onto the cheese. Was she aware of Claudio Daniel Troglia's invention of the same thing eleven years prior in Buenos Aires? We'll never know.

Nearly 2 billion people tune into the Live Aid concert on July 13. Organized in just ten weeks, it raises more than $125 million for famine relief in Ethiopia.

1985

THE START OF SELOSSE'S SOMETHING

GAINING THE NAME RECOGNITION OF DOM PÉRIGNON OR CRISTAL IN Champagne was out of the question for winemaker Anselme Selosse in the 1980s. His intention was never to build a global luxury brand, anyway. But there's no denying that Selosse's impact on Champagne has been as significant as any. Selosse started the grower Champagne movement— essentially sparkling wine's equivalent to microbreweries putting out craft beer. And like most small, independently owned businesses, Selosse obsessed over things like point of view and attention to detail rather than mass-market appeal. In fact, Selosse's style is not welcomed by the mass market at all. While many consider his wines the most distinctive of all Champagne, others deem them too avant-garde, or even faulty.

Selosse has released a dozen or so bottlings, but one wine has come to define his style more than any other. Substance, as it is known, is a chardonnay-based Champagne made using a perpetual blending technique called solera, which originated in the sherry region of Spain (see page 32). The idea here is that the blend results in the ultimate expression of a vineyard and its potential, showing the good, great, bad, and terrible vintages that happen over its lifetime.

Substance's solera was created in 1986. This Champagne is not meant to be light enough to drink before a meal or fresh enough to pair with fried chicken (which more conventional Champagne does surprisingly well). Substance is the opposite of the Blanc de Blancs, the 100 percent chardonnay-based Champagne most come to expect when popping open a bottle of bubbly. Rather, the combination of vintages and extended exposure to oxygen make a Champagne that is nutty, tealike, and round.

Whether you like it or not, you can't deny the impact of what Selosse started in 1986, especially considering his mentorship of some of Champagne's younger stars. Chartogne-Taillet, Jérôme Prévost, and Ulysse Collin have all worked under his supervision. Their wines do not necessarily reflect his style of winemaking, but they do embody his devotion to the craft of Champagne from vineyard to bottle, with or without the solera.

California farmer Mike Yurosek comes up with the idea of "baby" carrots as a way to sell those that are broken and misshapen. Carrot consumption increases by 30 percent within a year.

Nine months after discovering the wreck of the *Titanic*, a team from the Woods Hole Oceanographic Institute returns to capture it on film.

On April 26, the Chernobyl nuclear plant explodes. It is the worst nuclear disaster in history, releasing more than two hundred times the combined radiation of the bombs dropped on Hiroshima and Nagasaki.

1986

TRUST ME: IMPORTERS TO KNOW

Asking sommeliers how they tell whether the wine is good based on the label is like asking a child why they smeared peanut butter on their sibling. They can answer the question, but you won't necessarily know what to do with the information.

That said, one reliable heuristic found on any bottle outside of its country of origin is the name of the importer. Importers often specialize in a certain country or style of wine. They source from independent producers, and their selections show a through line of winemaking philosophy and standard of quality. Some importers have an instrumental impact on what the wine market looks like today—even if they're no longer in business, or even alive. Some also continue to discover wines from remote regions or emerging producers, then provide those selections to restaurants and retailers alike. The best importers are agents of good taste. You can trust those with the good stuff to lead you into the unknown.

French Wine
- Becky Wasserman
- Camille Rivière Selection
- Grand Cru Selections
- Kermit Lynch
- Martine's Wines
- The Sorting Table

Italian Wine
- Oliver McCrum
- Polaner Selections
- The Rare Wine Co.
- Rosenthal Wine Merchant
- Tradizione Imports

Natural Wine
- José Pastor Selections
- Louis/Dressner Selections
- Selection Massale
- Zev Rovine Selections

Champagne
- Grand Cru Selections
- Kermit Lynch
- Polaner Selections
- Skurnik Wines & Spirits

German Wine
- Sussex Wine Merchants
- Vom Boden

THE BEGINNING OF THE END

SPORTS HAVE ENTIRE ERAS OF GREATNESS: FOR TENNIS IN THE 2000s, the Williams sisters ruled. For basketball in the 1990s, the Chicago Bulls. Ice hockey is all about America in 1980. The list goes on. Not entirely dissimilarly, wine has short stints in which a region has perfect weather and great winemakers with the skills to hold up their end of the deal. Beginning in 1988 and for three years following, France's Rhône Valley had its moment.

The Rhône Valley runs along the Rhône River from the northernmost town, Côte-Rôtie, down to Cornas, encompassing the Northern Rhône region. Beyond that is the Southern Rhône Valley, a larger area best known for its subregion Châteauneuf-du-Pape. Even in the late '80s, producers in the region seemed like vestiges of another time. In contrast to the modern and technical winemaking that was coming in vogue and would thrive in the early '90s, Rhône producers were farmers, making wine from their family-owned vineyards as they had done for generations. Their methods were simple and pure—no new oak barrels and no desire to alter the taste away from savory and toward sweet.

But rustic was the opposite of cool, so in time, some local wineries changed their ways, trying to gain a foothold in the international market. Others were left to languish, including Marius Gentaz, Noël Verset, and Raymond Trollat. In all three instances, these namesake founders passed away leaving behind bottles—and posthumous fame—but no successors to their low-tech wine estates. It's only in hindsight that collectors have begun to realize what has been lost. Each of the three wineries, now closed, is now considered a benchmark in their respective regions of Côte-Rôtie, Cornas, and Saint-Joseph. Across the Rhône, the 1988 to 1991 bottles are now the most expensive. Bluntly, some are more worthy of the price tag than others, but scarcity is its own raison d'être. At the rate of consumption today, the work of these Rhône boys won't be around much longer. Even though we've acknowledged our errant ways, it's too late to go back to traditional methods and recover the magic of the late '80s, not least because of changing weather.

Nowhere is that statement more acute than in Châteauneuf-du-Pape, where the climate is now nearly Mediterranean. Though grapes have grown there since ancient times—the region got its name later when a series of popes moved in starting in 1309—and it was the first French AOC-designated region, it was not a household name outside of France until the '90s. Like your friend who just blows past personal boundaries, Châteauneuf is often just too intense. But for those four wonderful years, starting in 1988, the weather and the minimal-intervention philosophy conspired to produce delicate, nuanced Châteauneufs across the region. Unfortunately, though, that style, like the region's rustic philosophy, had

Physicist Nicholas Kurti and chemist Hervé This coin the term "molecular gastronomy" to describe the scientific study of cooking, unintentionally leading to a surfeit of foam in fine dining.

As a result of diet culture villainizing fat throughout the decade, combined low-fat and skim milk sales exceed those of whole milk for the first time.

Selinsgrove, Pennsylvania, sets the world record for the longest banana split. Coming in at 4.55 miles, made of 33,000 bananas and 2,500 gallons of ice cream, it holds the title for the next twenty-nine years until residents of Innisfail, Australia, celebrating the recovery of their hometown from a tropical cyclone, break it.

1988

the bad luck of being out of step with fashion, so Châteauneuf producers leaned away from it and toward the high-in-alcohol and borderline port-like wines that were super on trend. It was a commercially smart move—the big, punchy stuff, combined with the whimsical name, and the lusher, oakier expressions that producers started to experiment with were in lockstep with the market. Suddenly, in the '90s, Châteauneuf wasn't just a wine, it was a brand. But at what cost? Even as the pendulum swings back in favor of more nuanced wine, for most wineries in the region, it's too late. As the weather gets hotter, it gets harder and harder to prevent grenache, Châteauneuf's primary grape, from displaying its worst qualities (think: Costco sample chocolate-covered strawberry filled with rum).

Thankfully, there are a few exceptions to this enormous loss. Producers like Châteauneuf's Château Rayas and Domaine Auguste Clape from Cornas in the north still haven't wavered from the ideals of the late '80s, despite the pressures of notoriety and commercial success that have been unrelenting since the region's heyday. Rayas's greatness transcends both its region and its grape. In today's climate, it is astonishing that from 100 percent grenache, they are still able to make the delicate, peppery, and light reds they are known for. One secret to Rayas is their lack of intervention in the wines, but even more than that, it's their vineyard's dry and sandy soils that lend themselves to a nuanced version of grenache rather than an overblown one. You can find oceans of Châteauneuf-du-Pape, but only a few enchanted swimming holes' worth of Rayas, one of France's best wines and certainly the Southern Rhône's most supreme.

IF YOU SMELL WHAT HAUT-BRION IS COOKING

BEFORE DWAYNE "THE ROCK" JOHNSON WAS A MOVIE STAR, HE WAS A sports hero (well, a professional wrestler), and there's no denying that he's one of only a few who excels at both pursuits. Similarly, only a few winemakers make both red and white wines exceptionally. Most successful winemakers take a shot at trying the other color, but rarely does the attempt live up to the results they get with their main grape. Making red and making white are two different skill sets, as the fermentation and barrel aging require different knowledge.

Château Haut-Brion is known for their red wines in the Bordeaux region of Graves, and they've been around since the very beginning (see page 71). Declaring 1989 one of their best vintages ever is a contemporary point of view, but it objectively ranks near the top of their list of over four hundred years of vintages. One reason is that in 1989, both Haut-Brion red and Haut-Brion white were among Bordeaux's best wines of the vintage in their respective categories.

You'd think that if a year is good for red, it's good for white, too—but this is not always true. White grapes are almost always harvested earlier than red grapes, and the last few weeks before harvest begins are the most volatile. Fall weather can shake a vintage from glory to disgrace with just one bad storm. It's only when the weather is stable and on its very best behavior through the end of grape-growing season that a good white year might *also* be a good red year. This was the case in Graves in 1989, resulting in red and white Haut-Brions that both received perfect scores from critics and continue to age marvelously.

The Berlin Wall falls. So, too, does a seventy-four-year-long ban on beer in Iceland.

A fish distributor finally persuades the FDA to allow imports of fugu, the poisonous puffer fish whose toxin has no known antidote.

Tim Berners-Lee, a computer scientist working at the CERN particle physics lab, writes the proposal document that becomes the blueprint for the World Wide Web. His manager called his proposal "vague, but exciting," which turns out to be a pretty accurate summary of the internet.

1989

PART III

THE REIGN OF POINTS
(1990 TO 2008)

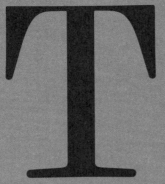

Think back. Waaaay back. I know it's tough to remember, but before social media caused our collective attention span to drop to under ten seconds, people read things on paper, like books and newspapers and magazines. One of those was the newsletter the *Wine Advocate*, which was created in 1978 by Robert Parker, a lawyer by profession, and America's first (and perhaps only) Famous Wine Guy™. Parker quite literally invented the 100-point quality scale for wine; using a simple calculation, he would declare a wine to be great or not so great. We hold many bottles in high regard simply because he said so. He was a consistent man: a great Parker vintage was almost certainly a red wine so dark it stained your teeth, high in alcohol (at least 14.5% ABV), and aged in new oak barrels, with notes of chocolate, prunes, and baking spices. Basically, he's a guy who wanted hot fudge sundaes with all the works. Whether or not you like that style, it was amazing to see dusty classification systems that had frozen a specific hierarchy of wine disrupted by a single simple idea. Instead of the Burgundy system that classified wines according to vineyard and the Bordeaux one that classified them by price, here was this American guy saying, "What if we just categorized them by taste?" That said, objectivity was not the name of the game here.

As mentioned, Parker's notoriety exploded with the lavish praise he heaped on 1982 Bordeaux. However, the distillation of wine analysis to a numeric score, and that score's impact on global wine prices, really set in around 1990. While any wine drinker today should respect what Parker achieved—and many do, as his point system is still widely used by other critics—they should also be aware that his scores don't account for the fact that, with time, wines change—for better *and* for worse. In many instances, a wine that started out as the dorky kid in high school goes on to become the boss. But few wines were rescored, and even when they were, it was the initial score that mattered to the market.

Still, critics are important, and for many wineries, receiving high points has been a game changer. Sassicaia's 100-point 1985 vintage trades for around $3,000 a bottle, while the 1984 and 1986 vintages go for around $500. The 1985 is inarguably superior, but its cost is also inarguably inflated. And in most instances, once a high-scoring wine, always a high-scoring wine. Seeking a high score on the first day of a wine's life shifted the way wines were made during the 1990s and early 2000s—few for the better and many for the worse.

Also during this period, in wealthier areas like Bordeaux and California, a market of consulting winemakers emerged. These academics instructed winemakers on the newer tools available to them—suggesting using a different strain of yeast, adding nutrients during fermentation, analyzing the chemistry of an unfinished wine to ensure it arrives at the intended ideal taste. The list of services goes on. Consultants like France's Michel Rolland worked with new wineries that wanted to launch as top contenders and old ones trying to achieve the tastes coming into popularity. Rolland is called a "flying winemaker," as he consulted for more than 150 wineries across the globe. Rolland had a recipe, and the end result was a consistent taste: fruity, clean, and bold. By no coincidence, Rolland's suggestions shifted wine toward Parker's preferred flavors, regardless of what the geology of a vineyard could (and perhaps should) produce.

The nineties and early aughts was an era of extremes. While some wines could have benefited from using new technologies to manage the surprising temperatures brought about by early-stage global warming, others could have left a bit more to the elements. In short, as new ideas clashed with standards of the past, and combined with the impact of climate change's early signs, many wines from these years taste uncertain, and a few, who kept their cool, prevailed.

GRAND AND GRACEFUL

THE PHRASE *VIGNERONS DE PÈRE EN FILS DEPUIS 1481* TRANSLATES TO "vine growers from father to son since 1481." That's quite a bold statement to lead with on a wine label. And the only winery in the world that can carry such a big stick is the Rhône Valley's Domaine Jean-Louis Chave.

As the most established landowners on the hill of Hermitage, Chave makes a substantial amount of wine. Both their Hermitage Blanc and Hermitage Rouge are as long-lived and age-worthy as any wines on the planet. The Rouge, the family's flagship wine, is 100 percent syrah from a variety of different plots along the Hermitage. Syrah is a dark grape that can produce big wines, but in the hands of Chave, it yields a certain grace; the wine is known for its distinct black pepper and lavender flavors. The unique blending of the independent parcels to determine a final concoction worthy of the family's reputation of excellence is their trademark. No pressure. So when the Chave family decided to make a special release of the Rouge in 1990, rest assured, the decision wasn't made impulsively to chase trends, nor was it an effort to capitalize on a landmark year. Cuvée Cathelin, as the bottling is known, is only released in special years when the annual blend of the different parcels offers a unique twist on Hermitage. Made just seven times since its inaugural release in 1990, it is exceedingly rare. Discerning whether a year will have Cathelin or only the Rouge is based on taste and feeling by the Chave family. In the unprecedented 1990 vintage, they found the flavor they'd been searching for.

While Chave is accredited as the longest-standing legend of the Rhône, Allemand is the fastest to rise to that stature. In 1990, new kid on the block Thierry Allemand started making wine under his own label. He had previously apprenticed for the famed Noël Verset, who, like Allemand, only made wine in Cornas, the most southern region for syrah in the Northern Rhône. The classic profile of Cornas is rich, dark, and broad. It can be those things, but in the hands of Allemand, who works the grapes with a graceful and light touch, it maintains a balance of delicate flavors. Thanks to him, this more tender style of making syrah has been adapted by younger regions and winemakers as well.

On February 11, Nelson Mandela is released from prison after being incarcerated for twenty-seven years for opposing apartheid in South Africa. The four-year-long negotiations to dismantle apartheid begin later this year.

After cutting through the last pieces of rock, the British and French diggers who had been working from their respective sides of the English Channel shake hands to celebrate. The Channel Tunnel, nicknamed "the Chunnel," is the first land connection between Great Britain and mainland Europe since the megaflood that formed the channel hundreds of thousands of years earlier.

Benazir Bhutto, prime minster of Pakistan, becomes the first modern head of government to give birth while in office. It's a girl.

1990

BABY GOT BLANC: NORTHERN RHÔNE WHITE WINE

While the best red wines of the Northern Rhône tame the grapes to preserve their elegance, most of the region's lesser-seen white wines are so floral and candied-fruit-flavored, they would serve better as plug-in air fresheners. The areas to avoid here are vast, but the ones to source are truly special: Hermitage Blanc from Chave and, above all others, Château-Grillet.

Chave's Hermitage Blanc is made from the grapes marsanne and roussanne. When they're young, they taste like you're slurping olive oil from the bottle, but imagine tinges of almond, apricot, and salt instead of salad dressing. Over time—even a century's length—they stay fresh and evolve into a mesmerizing mix of citrus, cardamom, and herbs. Granted, the taste is not for everyone. It can be jarring for those who drink the crisper, drier white wines of Chablis, Sancerre,

and even Burgundy. But trust that in around thirty years, a Hermitage Blanc and a quality French cheese will match as well as George and Amal.

The other notable spot is Condrieu, a single-producer region where Château-Grillet exclusively works with the floral and perfume-like viognier grape. When planted in rich soils, viognier can get so ripe and exotic that notes of dish soap start to permeate—most of it tastes like shampoo. It's often overpriced and always bad. But grown in this tiny region (ten acres in size; about ten thousand bottles are released annually), viognier is just different. Château-Grillet's old vines are on dramatic terraces built into the granite cliffs that surround the winery. This lighter soil yields grapes with a more delicate flavor. Château-Grillet isn't just the greatest viognier, it's greater than viognier.

LEROY MEANS BUSINESS

Lalou Bize-Leroy was born on third base. Her family has co-owned Domaine de la Romanée-Conti in Burgundy since 1942, and even before that, they operated the négociant business Maison Leroy in 1868. This is to say that the Leroy family has been entrepreneurial since the very idea existed. Their business model—buying finished wine from unnamed farmers to sell under their own name—was not unique. This "white-label" model still exists, but no one has pulled off prices as astronomical as Leroy's.

Lalou could have lived a cushy life just sitting back and collecting dividends from her ownership stake in these businesses. But in 1988, she decided to start making wine on her own. She formed Domaine Leroy after purchasing some vineyards in the area, as well as Domaine d'Auvenay, whose tiny number of vineyards were mostly devoted to white wine. Although the family had never made wine themselves, Lalou knew Burgundy as well as anyone else—and that knowledge propelled her to near-instant success.

If one vintage of the newly homemade Leroy wines reigned supreme, it was 1991. Burgundy's transition to organic farming was just taking off, and Lalou was at the forefront of preaching that the work in the vineyards was paramount to a great wine; indeed, her wines have been biodynamically farmed since day one. In 1991, the weather was not as sunny as the warm and powerful 1990 vintage, so the market, at first, pushed them to the side. (A vintage following a highly praised year tends to be overlooked simply because of the previous year's success. The same happened with 1983 Bordeaux following its massive hit in 1982.) While 1991 suffered for its timing at first, the market for these wines would eventually upstage the 1990 as they aged. Highlights of reds from Domaine Leroy in 1991 are Musigny, Richebourg, Chambertin, and Romanée-Saint-Vivant. In their youth, these wines were tart and crisp compared to the sweeter 1990, but that's exactly what has allowed them to mature more steadily—now a 1991 Leroy costs nearly double what a 1990 does. Is it twice as good? No. But is it better? Yes, and the Leroy family knows that. As long as they've known good wine, they've known good business—and for that, they deserve a nod, too.

Freddie Mercury, the three-octave voice of Queen, dies in London due to complications from AIDS, one day after revealing his diagnosis to the world.

The Honeycrisp, considered the first "brand name" apple, is introduced by researchers at the University of Minnesota.

The Cold War formally ends on December 26 when the Soviet Union votes to dissolve itself.

1991

MOON CYCLES AND MANURE: BIODYNAMIC WINE

"Biodynamic" is a pretty mainstream term for a pretty esoteric set of ideas. This type of farming is as much a scientific-spiritual philosophy as it is a farming practice, and it started with Austrian spiritualist Rudolf Steiner (the same guy who founded the Waldorf schools, if you're familiar). In 1924, in response to chemical agriculture, which was then all the rage, Steiner gave a lecture series outlining his belief that a farm is a living organism and agricultural practices should be about maintaining balance and working *with* nature rather than fighting against it. He knew his lectures were just a first draft and that he had a lot more work to do—but he died before he could refine his ideas. This unpolished lecture series is the biodynamic bible.

The core foundation of biodynamic farming is essentially identical to organic farming: no chemicals, use manure instead of industrial fertilizer whenever possible, and work with the ecosystem to ward off pests rather than using pesticides. Some practices it prescribes—like crop rotation and composting—make a ton of sense and have been a key part of farming since way back when. Planting and harvesting according to lunar cycles is also a very, very old concept: in ancient times, when calendars hadn't yet been standardized, the moon offered a way to track time, and therefore indicated when to plant. Other practices are loopier and lean more into the mystic, involving herbal preparations and cosmic forces and borderline occult rituals. (One involves burying a cow horn filled with manure at a specific time of year.)

Steiner developed his methods through meditation and clairvoyance, and we haven't seen any solid scientific studies on the effectiveness of biodynamic farming. In fact, in a recent paper, horticultural academics argued that "any effect attributed to biodynamic preparation is a matter of belief, not of fact." But winemakers claim they can objectively tell the difference between a grape grown biodynamically and one grown just organically. Which is why, even though biodynamic wasn't created as a philosophy exclusively for wine, the wine industry has adopted it more enthusiastically than any other.

In 1969, Eugène Meyer in Alsace was one of the first to do so, after becoming disenchanted with conventional methods when exposure to chemical spray damaged his optic nerve. The practice then spread to the Loire and east to Vouvray and finally to Burgundy, where Anne-Claude Leflaive led the charge. Now the trend is bigger than ever. The United States currently has the third most biodynamic wineries in the world, and the unofficial number is even larger than gets credited, since many opt out of the most occult bits. You know something's going on when Cristal—about as regal, pretentious, and non-hippie-dippie a brand as it gets—is marketing a biodynamic Champagne.

STARS ARE BORN

WHEN DOMAINE LEFLAIVE ACQUIRED A PIECE OF LAND IN THE GRAND cru vineyard Montrachet in the early '90s, Burgundy was still transitioning from the humble region it once was into the world's most valuable vineyard per acre, as it's known today. In hindsight, the purchase was an asset acquisition equivalent to buying shares of Microsoft the day before it went public.

Leflaive was already considered one of the most eminent white wine makers of France, so the land deal was befitting of their pedigree, but Anne-Claude Leflaive had only recently taken the helm of her family's namesake winery, with the help of Pierre Morey (see page 106), when the Montrachet purchase was finalized. She was not a winemaker, but she was obsessed with grape growing and farming. Leflaive slowly converted the entire property to biodynamics while sharing her insights with others: respect the land, and the better wine will come. Montrachet is the origin of many of the most widely considered greatest white wines of all time, but you'd be hard-pressed to find a better expression of this special dirt than the wines from the single barrel (that's only three hundred bottles) that Domaine Leflaive produces annually. The best of the best among these precious bottles is 1992. Glossed over for quality wines in other regions due to fatal rains, 1992 is a star in Burgundy.

While Leflaive was crafting one of France's most iconic white wines, Jean Philips and Heidi Peterson were in Napa Valley working on what would become America's most expensive red: Screaming Eagle. The two were just starting their careers. Jean, a real estate agent with an eye for vineyard plots, hadn't intended to create a celebrity wine. He bought the Screaming Eagle vineyard because he just had a great feeling about its potential. Jean then brought Heidi on board, who, at that point, was an up-and-coming winemaker.

In 1992, Napa Valley was just beginning to see a new boom, thanks to Robert Parker's influence. Parker could change the lives of winemakers, and he did so for Jean and Heidi when he awarded the inaugural vintage of Screaming Eagle a 99-point score. This vintage, and other more potent wines, quickly become the protagonists for Napa Valley's third act, aimed at decadence rather than subtlety. Screaming Eagle and others achieved bigger (and, according to some, better) wines by using new oak barrels and pushing the ripeness of their grapes to have sugar levels higher than those of the past. At the time, this combination was a revelation. Like scooping into a baked Alaska for the first time, those first sips of Screaming Eagle dropped jaws. Is it worth the price? No, but without a doubt, Jean and Heidi's intentions to make a great wine were pure.

Salsa sales overtake ketchup sales for the first time in the United States.

After President George H. W. Bush vomits on the prime minister of Japan during a formal state dinner, the Japanese coin a new word: *Bushusuru*, meaning "to vomit in public," or, more literally, "to do a Bush."

Composer Stephen Sondheim and author Wallace Stegner refuse their National Medal for the Arts awards to protest what they view as American censorship of the arts.

1992

CALIFORNIA LOVE

MANY GREAT INVENTIONS END UP SHROUDED IN CONTROVERSY: WHO did it first? Examples include calculus, the telephone, and cult California cabernet. For some, Screaming Eagle was the first to bring Beatles-like mania to the act of buying a bottle of American wine in 1992 (see page 145)—but for others, first up was either Harlan or Sine Qua Non.

Harlan, founded in 1990, prides itself on the consistency and purity of the small quantity of wine they produce every year. With the power and force unique to the best vineyards of Napa, Harlan is one of the few domestic wines found in the cellars of Francophile collectors. It was a top year for most California cabernets: mild weather conditions produced wines with the full body of the modern style but the savory flavors of the old-school greats. Upon initial release, though, these bottles weren't considered the all-stars they are today, dismissed as sharp and too light by some. With the benefit of time, Harlan's 1994 vintage has emerged as the highlight of the winery's history.

If Harlan is quiet and diligent, Sine Qua Non (SQN) is its opposite. In the same year, Manfred Krankl, an Angeleno restaurateur by way of Austria, started the loud, flashy winery. That first year, he made four-and-a-half barrels (around fifteen hundred bottles) of red from syrah and called it the Queen of Spades. Queen of Spades proved that the West Coast spectrum of grapes can go beyond cabernet and chardonnay. In addition to syrah, other Rhône Valley varieties like grenache and mourvèdre have found a home in the warm, arid vineyards of Ventura County near Los Angeles. If Napa looks to Bordeaux for inspiration, these wines aspire to be like the jammy and herbaceous wines of France's Southern Rhône region—like Châteauneuf-du-Pape (see page 127). But SQN has not tried to emulate the Old World at all, and Krankl made that clear beginning with his ostentatious presentation of Queen of Spades. Until 2021, when he seemingly tired of the exercise, Krankl created a new name and designed a new label for every single bottling. Some looked like playing cards; others like toys from a sex shop. With no inspiration from France at all, Krankl's unsubtle approach to marketing is one of the country's best: beginning with that first drop in 1994, SQN has sold out every year, and the wait to join their retail mailing list is years long. In this industry, it's both rare and unlikely that a wine named Ventriloquist with an abstract label will taste great, but Krankl has mastered ostentatiousness, spontaneity, *and* the challenges of making great wine.

Antarctica becomes the only continent from which dogs are banned due to concerns that they might transfer diseases to the seal population.

Riverdance, **Michael Flatley's** bedazzled Irish step dancing show, makes its world debut at this year's Eurovision Song Contest—as a mere intermission act.

Medaka, otherwise known as Japanese rice fish, become the first vertebrates to mate in space.

1994

COME SI DICE "ORANGE"? GRAVNER.

GRAVNER IS A SURNAME THAT, UNLIKE DA VINCI, ALIGHIERI, VERSACE, and Fellini, doesn't immediately indicate "Italian." But similar to those giants, Josko Gravner is equally important to his craft. Gravner is from Friuli in the far northeastern corner of Italy. Friuli is very much its own place—the dialect and culture there relate as much to its eastern border with Slovenia as to any neighboring region of Italy—and its wines speak to that. Gravner is the pioneer not only of the region, but also of the wine world at large, thanks to his dedication to orange wine. He wasn't the first to make orange wine, but he was the one to bring it back.

Gravner had mostly been making classic white wines throughout the 1980s. They were fruity and floral—good, but commonplace. A trip to the country of Georgia changed all that. He saw that the technique of aging wine in *qvevri*—huge clay containers buried in the ground—was still favored over stainless-steel tanks, and began to shift his winery in Friuli toward that style in 2001. Over time, he also moved the practices in his winery and vineyards in the low-intervention direction. Now Gravner's vineyards are full of life other than grapes; they sound like a bird sanctuary.

In 1996, Gravner released a blend of grapes called Breg that would be his first commercial sale of orange wine. It was received with anger and disgust. The wild flavors were too much of a departure from the ultra-clean and precise white wines of the rest of the country. At a time when the Italian market was praising watery, more minimalist whites, Gravner's Breg was full-on Jackson Pollock. Since then, Gravner's orange wines have continued to evolve. Some grapes, like pinot grigio, are no longer used, and the length of time they spend aging in the amphorae changes. One constant is that Gravner's orange wines are unlike any other.

Dolly the sheep, named after Dolly Parton, is born at the Roslin Institute in Edinburgh, Scotland—she is the first mammal cloned from an adult cell.

For April Fools' Day, Taco Bell takes out a full-page ad in several major newspapers announcing it has purchased the Liberty Bell and renamed it the Taco Liberty Bell in order to pay down the national debt.

What does a gorilla want for her twenty-fifth birthday? A box of scary rubber snakes and lizards, apparently. Or at least that's what Koko, the gorilla famous for her ability to use sign language, asks for—and receives.

1996

WHAT'S OLD IS NEW AGAIN: ORANGE WINE

Orange wine has been around for many thousands of years, but it only hit the mainstream in the past couple decades, thanks to our friend Josko Gravner. In other words, it's like kale: after a five-thousand-or-so-year hiatus, it has come back with a vengeance. "Orange" wine, now made all over the world from almost every white grape from muscat to chardonnay, is the same thing as skin-contact or macerated wine—and this is how you may see them grouped. While the terminology (confusingly) differs, these wines are gaining bigger and bigger footholds on wine lists and in wine stores.

Orange wine is made from white grapes left to ferment in their skins long enough to extract a rich flavor that you won't find in wine made in the classic style. It's basically the inverse of rosé. While rosé is a red wine made like a white wine, orange wine is a white wine made like a red wine. Traditionally, white grapes are crushed, and the juice is immediately separated from the skins. But when the juice is left in contact with the skins and seeds, it absorbs their color, becoming darker over time. Pinot grigio or sauvignon blanc might start out nearly clear or lemon-colored, but after a few hours (or months, depending on a producer's preferred style), they come out in varying shades of orange. The extended maceration not only imparts color, it also gives the wine body—as well as deep flavors ranging from nuts and apricots to that of a sour-style beer. That's why if traditional white wine is lemonade, orange wine is kombucha: they're both cold and refreshing drinks, but the former tastes familiar even as it varies between blends, and the latter is always a bit funky and spans a wide range of tastes. Some age well, and others expire as fast as milk.

SMOOOOOTH

WHEN A NEW HIGH-BUDGET HOLLYWOOD FILM DEBUTS, THE MANUFAC-tured level of excitement that accompanies it seems to imply it's got a built-in nod from the Academy. The wine industry does the same after a particularly great harvest, announcing: *the greatest vintage of all time is on the way!* In 1997, Italians doubled down on their celebrating. Coincidentally (or perhaps not), a long run of lackluster years had passed since the great 1990, at least according to critics. And at the time, these critics preferred wines that had softer and richer flavors from day one. Indeed, this is the period when the term "smooth" emerged as a subjective way to denote a wine's drinkability. It's commonly used to describe wines with a hot chocolate–like texture, which tend to be big and boozy. Italy in 1997 was as smooth as they come.

Some of the vintage's biggest hypebeasts were from international grapes in Tuscany, like Ornellaia, Solaia, and Tignanello. In Barolo, the stars (applauded then, but no longer considered worthy today) were Ceretto Barolo Bricco Rocche and Roberto Voerzio Barolo Brunate, the first ever to receive a 100-point score.

The hype Italians heaped on the 1997 vintage led to a boom in demand that endured for a while. In turn, restaurants raised the prices of a 1997 over a 1998, and especially over a 1996. Customers would explicitly ask for a 1997 as if to say their favorite fish was caviar and their favorite meat was foie gras. The hype lasted for about a decade, which isn't that long when it comes to wine. Indeed, bottles of 1997 have aged as gracefully as a boy band.

After a thirty-six-year ban, it's once again legal to give someone a tattoo in New York City. Officials claim the 1961 rule had been instituted because of a hepatitis B outbreak, but others think it was more about cleaning up the city before the '64 World's Fair.

"Wannabe" by the Spice Girls reaches number one on the Billboard charts, and the world meets Beyoncé Knowles when Destiny's Child releases their first hit single, "No, No, No."

Stanford PhD students Larry Page and Sergey Brin register the domain google.com to house the research project that they had initially named "Backrub."

1997

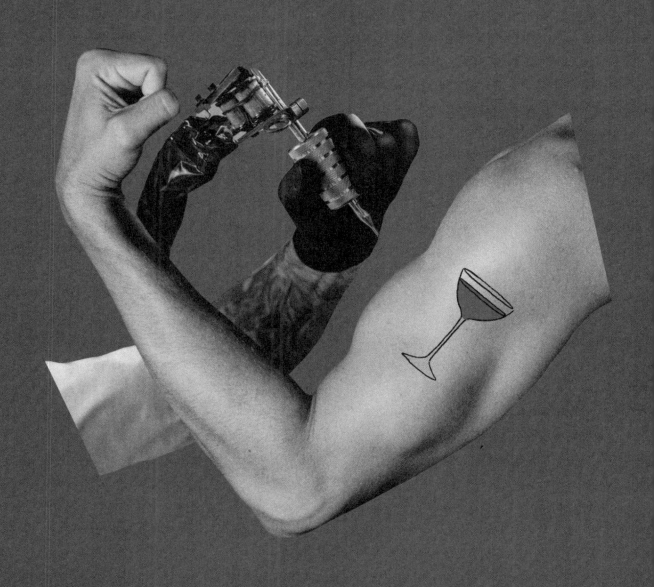

THE UNDERGROUND

Italian wine did not put its best foot forward in the early-2000s era. It seemed like a good idea for a second, but in hindsight, it's just not that cool. At the time, internationally known Italian wines were made to taste like the then-in-vogue reds of Northern California. We can't blame the winemakers for producing wine that people wanted to buy—money talks. But thankfully, around the same time—in regions more remote than Tuscany and Barolo—some winemakers were staying true to their roots and producing some of the country's most celebrated bottles.

One of those places was Mount Etna. As a wine region, Mount Etna is as old as it gets; the active volcano on the island of Sicily has been home to grapes for millennia. Later, chardonnay, merlot, and syrah were planted there thanks to their easy assimilation onto wine shop shelves. These grapes were used primarily for bulk production—that is, wines drunk only for the fact that they were wet and contained alcohol. But eventually, in a collaboration with the Benanti family, a young winemaker named Salvo Foti said, "Hold up, we can do something better." Their endeavors began in 1990, and by 2001 the quality was high enough to land Etna on the international map of good wine.

Under the Benanti label, Foti and the family made wines from local Etna varieties. The white, Pietramarina, is made from carricante, a crisp, savory white grape that tastes like top-tier Chablis on its best days and a simple thirst-quenching Italian white on its worst. The reds, Serra della Contessa and Rovittello, are from the nerello grape, which produces wines more comparable to pinot noir and Barolo than the dark, rich reds common in the Italian south. Foti's move started a renaissance for Etna, and then for the rest of Sicily as well. Other producers, like Calabretta and Marc de Grazia of Tenuta delle Terre Nere have successfully followed suit, making wines whose sense of place could be nowhere other than Sicilian turf.

While Benanti embraced the classic approach to winemaking—albeit using indigenous grapes—Frank Cornelissen, a Belgian-born winemaker who established an estate on Etna in 2001, was entirely avant-garde. For winemaking inspiration, he looked backward rather than forward, producing wines from nerello grapes without using any vine treatments during the growing season or adding sulfur to his final product. Cornelissen is credited with bringing this extreme style of natural wine to the Italian masses and beyond. His impact has been as monumental as the volcano on whose slopes he still makes wine today.

Back on the mainland, in the south-central region of Abruzzo, the winery Valentini was making red, white, and a shocking style of rosé from native varieties of trebbiano and Montepulciano. These are two of Italy's most widely planted grapes, and they produce some of Italy's

Venus and Serena Williams face each other in the finals of the US Open, becoming the first sisters to compete for a Grand Slam championship since Maud Watson defeated her older sister, Lilian, at Wimbledon in 1884.

Apple releases iTunes and the first-generation iPod.

Italy's Leaning Tower of Pisa reopens to the public after nearly twelve years of stabilization efforts, which straightens the lean by over a foot. Engineers believe they did enough to get the nearly 850-year-old tower to reach at least its one thousandth birthday.

2001

most consistently mediocre wines—except in Valentini's hands. So while Valentini's annual production is just a sliver of the grapes' total volume, it represents almost all their potential. Valentini's style stood in opposition to just about every trend in wine at the time. The reds are dark and umami; the whites are cloudy and rich—the epitome of a salty white wine. And the rosé, known locally as cerasuolo, tastes more like a light natural red wine than a traditional rosé. Along with the wines of Tiberio and Emidio Pepe (two other Abruzzian producers), Valentini stood its course during Italy's transition, and has prevailed as one of the nation's lesser-known icons. Their wines are now some of the most celebrated on the planet.

Italy's smallest wine icon, at least in terms of volume produced, is Miani, based in the northeastern region of Friuli. Miani makes a couple of barrels of red every year, but their powerful white wines from local grapes like friulano, malvasia, and ribolla gialla are what collectors seek. Friuli is a confusing region to define, but the wines of Miani do it the most justice. Their unique recipe draws inspiration from Burgundy, using small oak barrels to age the wines before bottling. The operation is impossible to scale, not because the vineyards are scarce, but because the owner, Enzo Pontoni, tends them like bonsai trees. Using grapes not usually believed capable of producing noteworthy wines, he gently coaxes out texture, richness, and longevity. Pontoni's white wines are exponentially more interesting than most other Italian white wines, the blandest of them all being pinot grigio. In 2001, pinot grigio still reigned as the ruler of Italian whites, but this year marked a distinct turning point for the quality of vino bianco as a whole.

WATER WINE: PINOT GRIGIO

In the wine world, pinot grigio is the equivalent of vodka. It's a workhorse for the larger industry and a gateway for less experienced consumers. The grape is easy to grow, and turning it into wine is speedy and inexpensive, with no required aging period. For this reason, you'll see pinot grigio released as early as rosé—six to nine months after the grapes are harvested. A few examples are worthy of respect, but most bottles are forgettable. After all, its purpose is to be uncomplicated and neutral in flavor.

Due to the overcommercialization and industrial farming of pinot grigio, very few emerging winemakers devote their time to the grape. The stuff that dominates supermarket shelves is still made in the style of the 1980s to early 2000s: light, neutral, and cheap. While drinking an ice-cold (or even ice-filled) glass of pinot grigio isn't an evil act, be warned: a lot of it is bad!

If your heart is set on pinot grigio, look for these sommelier-approved producers:

- Dalia Maris
- Venica & Venica
- Vignai Da Duline

If you want something that goes down just as easy but you're up for expanding your palate, look for these grapes:

- Falanghina
- Fiano di Avellino
- Friulano
- Greco di Tufo
- Verdicchio
- Vermentino

LA ROMANÉE REBOOT

IN BURGUNDY, THE PRECISE LOCATION OF ONE'S PROPERTY CAN BE THE difference between having multigenerational prosperity and being stuck envying your big shot next-door neighbor. More so than in any other region, the specificity of each plot of land's exposure to the sun, its soil makeup, and its exact elevation are what set apart good from priceless. Also more so than in any other region, this land has no secrets; it has been studied for thousands of years, so the really good stuff is known by all. It's now near impossible to acquire any of the upper-echelon vineyards, as strict laws protect the area, both restricting development and limiting who can invest in it. So how *does* change happen in this historic region? Slowly.

At one point, the Liger-Belair family owned La Tâche and La Romanée, the Burgundy vineyard equivalents of the *Mona Lisa* and *Salvator Mundi*. But after the family patriarch passed away in 1924, followed by his widow in 1931, the couple's ten children found their inheritance in jeopardy. The complex laws of that time stipulated that such an inheritance was to be divided equally among the heirs, and also required those heirs to have reached eighteen, the legal age of adulthood. Tragically, two of the ten children were minors, and in 1933, the government forced the land into public auction. Two of the Liger-Belair heirs—Michel and his brother Just, a priest—joined together to buy a few of the vineyards, including the entirety of La Romanée, which produces one of the greatest single-vineyard wines in the world, both then and now. For a time, the vineyards Just and Michel bought back were leased to the mediocre and mammoth Bouchard winery. Two generations later, Michel's grandson, Louis-Michel Liger-Belair, completed degrees in engineering and oenology. Only after that did his father, Henry, a military general, permit him to return to the idyllic village of Vosne-Romanée to reclaim the vineyards from the hands of their longtime lessee, a dream of his. Louis-Michel's first release under the family name came in 2002. Since then, as if making up for nearly centuries of lost time, Louis-Michel has returned the family name to the highest level of winemaking in the region.

Euro coins and banknotes are introduced on January 1, beginning the most ambitious currency changeover in history.

President George W. Bush approves Yucca Mountain as the country's nuclear waste dump site, and planners scramble to figure out how to warn future generations not to dig there. Nevada eventually pushes back—and we're still not sure what to do with our radioactive junk.

The era of Ryan Seacrest's ubiquity kicks off with *American Idol*'s debut.

2002

HOT RODS

UNTIL THIS POINT, THE MOST CRITICALLY ACCLAIMED VINTAGES CAME from hot years (see page 61). Hot years were "the best" simply because in cold years, their inverse, grapes couldn't ripen enough to achieve optimal taste. But how hot is too hot? In 2003, we found out. This year, every heat record was shattered, causing chaos throughout the Old World wine regions of Europe. The harvest, which began before September, was the earliest on record. For the first time, people began to seriously consider the effects of climate change on the flavor of wine.

Heat creates a bulky, uniform flavor that leaves no space for the expression of subtleties, and most of the wines resulting from the spike were dismissed immediately. It didn't help that this year was also the peak of Robert Parker's influence. The increase in alcohol naturally pushed all 2003 wines toward Parker's preferred profile—California-style rich and jammy—and winemakers, even European ones, didn't shy away. For most, it wasn't a good look; after all, the easiest way to throw shade at a European wine is to say it tastes Californian.

While many hope this vintage is long forgotten, some people—and some regions—wear that excessively sun-kissed glow well. Bordeaux, having found self-confidence in bigger wines, is one of those.

The vintage still has a stain on it—most collectors don't want to touch a 2003—but if you find a bottle from one of the below, the flavor can still be savored. These Bordeaux producers are the highest-praised and most powerful wines of the vintage:

- Château Ausone
- Château Lafite Rothschild
- Château Latour

The supersonic Concorde, which could make a transatlantic crossing in less than three hours, flies from New York City to London for the last time.

After thirteen years, the Human Genome Project is complete, having sequenced 99 percent of our genetic blueprint with 99.99 percent accuracy.

Narinder Badwal, a 7-Eleven franchise owner, is thrilled when he learns he sold the winning ticket to the California lottery and is entitled to a $250,000 commission. His day gets even better when he realizes he sold the winning ticket, worth more than $49 million, to *himself*. He and his wife celebrate by giving free Slurpees to their customers.

2003

THAT'S DARK

SUMMER 2004 WAS CONSISTENTLY CLOUDY AND COOL. COLD VINTAGES produce acidic wines that are tart in flavor. For white wines, that was a good thing, producing acidic wines with an ability to age while still remaining zesty and refreshing (see page 166). For reds, the weather made for very light wines, which some regions even deemed faulty due to prevalent flavors of green herbs and grass. Cold-vintage reds can be uncomfortable to drink if you're accustomed to the sweet and supple flavors of higher-alcohol wines coming from warmer vintages. It might be like biting into a peach you thought would be juicy and sweet, and instead finding it tart and rock-hard. But just as the peach only needed time to ripen, 2004 reds, like those from Burgundy, just required a bit more time in the bottle. Two decades later, these wines—previously avoided by collectors—now represent some of the great values in the region.

When a vintage is declared to be a bad one, prices stay low for years; a bottle of 2004 could cost half as much as the same bottle of 2005 simply because of the reputation of the vintage. But one producer's 2004 wines that certainly aren't going for less are those of René Engel. This vintage is the last from the winery, which was established in 1919 and passed through three generations of winemakers before being sold to French billionaire François Pinault. Engel's Burgundies are known for their rich and hearty style. In a vintage like 2004, where savory and herbaceous flavors are already turned up, Engel's work strikes a balance. His exceptional celebrity is largely a posthumous effect, but this small and humble winery made some great wines nonetheless. The 2004 vintage is not their best, but as the last vintage of a long family legacy, it was certainly a delicious and respectable way to close.

While the legacy of Engel ended honorably, the legacy of some of Italy's most recognized producers of Brunello ended in controversy. Brunello shouldn't be such a big wine in the same way that Lance Armstrong shouldn't have so much stamina. According to the laws of the Brunello di Montalcino DOCG (see page 108), sangiovese, the native grape in Tuscany, must be the only grape in a wine for it to bear "Brunello di Montalcino" on its label. In contrast to the full and rich wines that were fetching the highest prices in the early aughts, sangiovese makes wine that is pale in color and tart in flavor, like pinot noir; however, in the hands of traditionalist producers, sangiovese's delicate flavors have levels of nuance that can compete with the greatest wines of the world. But commercially minded and decidedly non-traditionalist producers wanted a shortcut to international fame. In 2004, wineries like Argiano, Antinori, Banfi, and Frescobaldi suddenly came out with the most decadent Brunello ever, full of chocolaty, jammy, oaky flavors. The opulent wines were quite literally unbelievable, and experts across the globe questioned them, leading to

Harvard sophomore Mark Zuckerberg launches The Facebook from his dorm room.

"The One Where They Say Goodbye": *Friends* films its final episode. The cast is so emotional after their pre-curtain bow, their makeup must be redone before filming begins.

The first commercially successful e-cigarette, developed by Hon Lik, a Chinese pharmacist, goes on sale. Earlier models, designed as far back as the 1920s, never caught on.

2004

an international investigation in 2008. The investigation shed light on the fact that like those Tour de France cyclists, Brunello was doping: producers were injecting artificial coloring and using grapes with bigger flavors and darker hues to fabricate more richness than the wine should inherently have.

Meanwhile, the *real* wines of Montalcino had a very successful vintage. Lesser-known producers who had long been on the scene, like Poggio di Sotto, Il Paradiso di Manfredi, Salvioni, and Cerbaiona, made some of the best wines in the history of their land. Theirs were on the lighter, classic—authentic—side of the spectrum. At the same time, new wineries like Stella di Campalto and Pian dell'Orino emerged as the next generation of exceptional Montalcino producers. Today, their 2004 and proceeding vintages are some of the most sought-after wines in the world. With a balance of subtlety and power, they have a unique sense of place and great aging potential. This vintage did not need to exaggerate its flavors; if a 2004 is anything other than dried cherries, herbs, and sun-dried tomato, you can assume it is not an authentic Brunello.

THE TASTE OF HEAT: CLIMATE CHANGE

Extreme weather, such as hailstorms, can wipe out a whole year's crop, and fires can make wines taste like an old motel room. But natural disasters aside, steadily rising temperatures have already fundamentally changed the taste of wine. Since 2003, the temperature has only continued to creep up (2022 was literally melt-the-runway hot in London)—and winemakers have had to learn to adapt to their new reality and accept that past a certain point, their wine will never taste the same way it used to.

In some places, where the weather had been too cold, that's been a good thing: England is now producing pretty good sparkling wines, and Canada, Vermont, and Patagonia are getting into the business. But in regions where the weather was once perfect, the excess heat and sun are turning grapes into raisins, and wine is becoming heavier, boozier, and blindingly sweet. Previously balanced, graceful wines are now verging on fortified territory. In arid, sun-drenched Châteauneuf-du-Pape, for instance, certain producers are having to strip alcohol out of reds that had been praised for being super hedonistic. And in Napa, which was a cool-climate region the last time crop tops were in, we will likely never see a wine below 13% ABV again.

So how are winemakers adapting? Many are picking grapes at night or in the very early morning when acidity is highest. Some are experimenting with higher elevation. Sunshades help, but they're expensive. Changing the orientation of the vines can also be useful (that sweet southern exposure that your houseplants love is now something to be avoided), as can pruning in such a way that the leaves form their own sunshade. Some winemakers are grafting vines onto drought-resistant roots. Others—*ahem*, industrial producers—are experimenting with electrodialysis, which can increase acidity, and novel strains of yeast that produce less alcohol.

But mitigation has its limits. In Burgundy, the regulatory institute approved what might have been unthinkable just a few years ago: the use of new grapes in the blend to help the wine stay more balanced. It's just an experiment for now—officials will revisit the varieties in ten years and drop any that aren't making the cut. Regardless of which way the experiment goes, the very idea of it is a taste of what's to come.

THE GOOD DIE YOUNG: WHITE WINE'S AGING PROBLEM

Though red wine is normally what you think of when you imagine someone dredging a dusty bottle out the cellar (and for good reason—the stuff that makes red wine red offers protection against many of the ravages of time), white wine can age, too. Well, usually. Sometimes it doesn't—and no one knows why.

The mystery began in the early 2000s when collectors, excited to try what were supposed to be two sublime vintages of white Burgundy—'95 and '96—were horrified to discover something had gone extremely wrong. These wines, which were supposed to age for twenty to thirty years, were lifeless after not even a decade. Dark, oily, flat, bitter. They tasted like cooked vegetables and beeswax. Wine industry people labeled the issue "premox" or premature oxidization, but no one knew what was causing it.

Premox went beyond the '95 and '96 vintages, and it wasn't limited to white Burgundy, or to France, or even to Europe. The issue began appearing in bottles from California to Australia, affecting sweet and dry, sparkling and still wines alike. Some estimate the problem to have ravaged as many as 50 percent of bottles in a particularly bad year. (Around 2014, rumors began to swirl that premox had started afflicting red wines, too, but that's less well-documented.)

Even as scientists and producers began investing time and money into research, the cause still eluded them. The number of theories is dizzying. Some believe it was the switch from mechanical presses to gentler hydraulic presses around 1995. Others point to global warming, since overripe grapes lack certain protective compounds. Others still blame excess stirring of the wine, an ancient technique called bâtonnage. Another theory is that as consumers became more conscious about what they were putting into their bodies, some producers stopped using pesticides in the fields, leading to an overgrowth of grasses, which competed with vines for water. Stressed vines don't produce enough natural antioxidants. Health-conscious producers also added less sulfur to their wines, and in the absence of adequate levels of this antioxidant and preservative, wine has almost no protection. Finally, many blame the corks, pointing to premox variance within crates. As global demand for wine boomed in the mid-'90s, cork makers struggled to keep up, and quality dropped. Some vignerons, trying to kill the fungus that causes cork taint, created another problem by washing corks in hydrogen peroxide, which, many suspect, then mixed with the wine and started an oxidative chain reaction.

Now, more than two decades on from premox's first mention in the press, the crisis has abated somewhat. The precise cause still remains elusive, but producers have adapted their techniques based on whichever of the above theories they subscribe to—a return to mechanical presses, higher sulfur rates, screw caps, artificial corks—and the percentage of premoxed bottles has decreased. Some even report that bottles in cases that had been oxidized now taste great again (though science has yet to prove that reverse oxidation in wine is possible).

DOWN THE DRAIN

BY 2006, THE AMERICAN WINE MARKET HAD CLIMBED TO UNPRECE-dented levels. There was a new type of collector in town—one whose budget was supported by a Wall Street expense account and a bull market flush with cash. Young bottles of California cabernet were selling for $1,000 a pop, and the wine auction industry's revenue topped $30 million over the course of days. Wine turned from a quiet luxury into an essential guest at the dinner table for the newly wealthy in America.

This year was also pivotal for the transition from the big, high-alcohol wine styles praised by critics to renewed demand for old-school and low-intervention methods. You might even say it was the start of today's natural wine craze (see page 182). No wine embodies this transition better than that of Gianfranco Soldera, which straddles both worlds—delighting the points-obsessed and the craft-obsessed.

Soldera started his winery on a piece of property called the Case Basse in the heart of Montalcino, Italy. It's well known that he was not an easy man, but his relentless nature translated into the highest-quality wine, which combined the delicate and herbaceous aromas of sangiovese with a supple but refreshing taste. Soldera's personality was also, however, what caused a disgruntled employee to seek revenge against him in the way that would hit hardest.

Brunello di Montalcino needs ample aging time to refine its power into an approachable drink; it must rest in wooden vessels for a minimum of three years, and Soldera extended that aging even further. This meant that all the product from six vintages was being stored in the winery at once. His employee knew this, and also knew that Soldera purposefully lived without technology—including an alarm system. The proud Soldera, who had declared he would only ever drink his own wine, woke one cold morning to find that every barrel he'd made from 2007 to 2012 had been poured down the drain in the floor of his winery in the middle of the night. Worst of all, this tragedy occurred in the late years of his life. The 2006 Soldera Brunello di Montalcino is the last of its kind, and although Soldera did go on to make a small amount of wine before passing away in 2019, he never again produced a vintage under the Brunello di Montalcino label.

2006

IT'S WHAT'S INSIDE THAT COUNTS

MOST OF THE HEAVYWEIGHT PRODUCERS WHO WERE MAKING GREAT wine in the early 1900s have struggled to maintain both quality and relevance over time. Sure, these bigwigs may have had the best land, but over the intervening century, innumerable younger winemakers in Bordeaux, Burgundy, and Champagne have proven that a good wine isn't just the result of having top vineyards: a talented vigneron is required to make sure good grapes don't turn to swill. Equally, many of these major wineries, despite having made good wine for over a hundred years, have learned that there are plenty of reasons to fail: Maintaining quality is a grind. Doing better costs more. New weather patterns have changed the game. Drinkers' tastes have transformed.

But in 2008, one of those heavyweight wineries—the 175-year-old Champagne house Krug—outperformed in its class. Krug's main bottling is called Grand Cuvée. Released every year, it's a multi-vintage blend (see page 32) of up to twenty years of different vintages. Its overall style is on the rich and creamy end of the Champagne flavor spectrum. However, every so often, when the harvest is of high enough quality that it offers more on its own than it would contribute to the blend, Krug releases a vintage wine. From 1990 to 2022, only ten were released, and the 2008 is of such impeccable quality that even those who frown at the extravagance of Krug will smile with a glass in their hand.

Krug wasn't the only famed release of 2008—though it might have been the only one that deserved its fame based on what was *inside* the bottle. This year, the marketing department of the Bordeaux winery Lafite Rothschild etched the Chinese character for the number eight onto the bottle. Eight is considered the luckiest number in China, representing wealth, fortune, and prosperity. All those words can indeed describe the success of the 2008 Lafite: with the addition of the adornment on the package, its prices rose 20 percent. The wine itself wasn't so great—but the campaign sure did prove successful.

The term "mansplaining" takes off after Rebecca Solnit's essay "Men Explain Things to Me" describes the phenomenon precisely.

Cheap credit and lax lending standards lead to the 2008 financial crisis, the worst economic downturn since the Great Depression. At least there's no Prohibition to contend with this time.

Deep inside a sandstone mountain, the Global Seed Vault opens in the remote Arctic Svalbard region of Norway. The vault is the world's insurance against both manmade and natural disasters. The first withdrawal is made in 2015, to replant seeds lost due to the Syrian Civil War.

2008

PART IV

THE CURIOUS AGE
(2009 TO PRESENT)

If drinking wine was once about quantifying the prestige and blatant wealth of both the product and the drinker—that pinkie-up, swirling-a-giant-glass vibe—it seems only natural that the next generation would obsess over the underground and the unknown. This is the time of caring about exactly which farm your butter comes from, the revival of vinyl, and bucking tradition by wearing sneakers to the fine-dining spot that's been on your bucket list. A renewed focus on exploration has emerged—and for wine, this has meant questioning the value of those wines long deemed "the greats." The supremacy of curiosity over canon in this era has changed the way wine lists look, brought more wine to more corners of the world, and made wine more accessible to different communities and cultures. Never before has a small winery high in the mountains of France seen its wines in an exceptional restaurant in Mexico City.

Many of these lesser-known producers have social media to thank for their success. You once had to subscribe to Robert Parker's newsletter or, even worse, buy a copy of *Wine Enthusiast* to find out what the pros were drinking. Now you can learn about wines between perusing the latest trends in couches and looking at pics of your friend's new puppy. Add that to the rising numbers of both exceptional importers and exceptional wine bars, and we're giving away access for free.

While drinking old wine is—and always will be—an opportunity worth jumping at, the informed, respectful, and passionate work of today's younger winemakers is equally satisfying. Some rookie producers are becoming legit legends overnight, and the old guard is quickly being forgotten. Consumers today have neither cellars nor collections. Some of the best wines of the moment are made to drink now, and they don't need to cost a month's rent. At the end of the day, the best wine is the one you're having a good time drinking, right?

Don't let your guard down, though: thanks in part to technological advances and a surge in consumption, there's also more bad wine out there than ever before. On the record, most celebrity-endorsed wines and those sold in a can aren't on the market because their producers love the craft—they're just riding the wave of a booming business.

The acceleration of climate change has also challenged this generation in new and unprecedented ways. Hailstorms destroy entire annual crops all too frequently. Fires taint the flavor of wine the way campfire smoke clings to a wool sweater. And above all, the heat has irreversibly morphed the flavors of entire regions from quiet elegance into massive beast. From the eighties through the early aughts, consumers were most impressed by the power of big wines. Now the obsession is with acidity, freshness, and lightness. Instead of jammy and buttery, consumers seek out earthy and salty. And just as some wines ultimately became too big with flavors that were impressive but not delicious, as this trend progresses, some wines are now too light, too tart, too savory. In both instances, too much effort toward chasing a badge has proven to be in poor taste. (Besides, it's a losing battle: trends change every season.) The best producers avoid flavor trends altogether, putting their heads down to make the best possible product, full stop.

This period of great curiosity, exploration, and broadening tastes is reason to celebrate. But it would be foolish to claim which wines are already deserving of tributes equivalent to those that survived wars, especially as tastes continue to evolve. So, as we discuss more recent vintages—the now—we'll talk a bit less about specific bottlings and more broadly about new styles and lesser-known regions that have already risen to global obsession. Old and new, you can find a lot of delicious wine out there. Stay curious, and you won't go wrong.

SISTER ACT

LIKE INFLUENCER BIOS ON SOCIAL MEDIA, IN BURGUNDY, YOU'LL find many winery names adjoined by hyphens: Gagnard-Delagrange, Fontaine-Gagnard, Lamy-Pillot, Méo-Camuzet—the double-barreled list goes on. You'll also find the same last name shared among multiple wineries. In that instance, the winery name is the result of a split within a family, such as a cousin or sibling striking off to do their own thing. Don't be fooled by the similarity in names: Thibault Liger-Belair makes very different wine from Domaine du Comte Liger-Belair, just as Olivier Leflaive makes very different wine from Domaine Leflaive. The same cannot be said of Domaine Mugneret-Gibourg, Domaine Georges Mugneret, and Domaine Georges Mugneret-Gibourg.

In 1933, André Mugneret and his wife, Jeanne Gibourg, established Domaine Mugneret-Gibourg in Vosne-Romanée. Their son, Dr. Georges Mugneret, worked for the family business and grew it through the 1980s, renaming it Domaine Georges Mugneret. When he passed away in 1988, his wife, Jacqueline, took control of the winery, which she transferred to their daughters, Marie-Christine and Marie-Andrée Mugneret, upon her retirement in 2009.

Out of respect for the family business they inherited, the sisters changed its name again, christening it Domaine Georges Mugneret-Gibourg, bringing together their grandparents' names with their father's in homage to the multiple generations that had blessed them with such an inheritance. And, as it often does, the subtle name change represented a shift in quality, too. (In this case, that shift—from very good to outstanding—had slowly been happening for years.) The same year Marie-Christine and Marie-Andrée assumed full control, their wines reached global fame. The 2009 vintage came at the exact right time, as the American market, rebounding from the Great Recession, was seeking more Burgundy than ever before. The vintage was bountiful and had a generosity of flavor that made it approachable for this wider international market and easy to drink young.

Today, Marie-Christine and Marie-Andrée are at the top of the hierarchy of all producers of Burgundy. Their style is smooth and perfume-like. In this region, all wines have the ability to be light and crowd-pleasing, but certain decisions in the winemaking process can steer them toward austere and rustic. One of the hard parts of navigating the producers of Burgundy is that two bottles from the same village, grape, and vintage can be so very different. Indeed, the success of a good Burgundy is in the hands of the winemaker—and in the case of these sisters, that has meant an extra pair of talented hands. Deservedly, they've brought their family's name—in all its variations—to stardom.

A truck in Utah accidentally dumps 40,000 pounds of hamburger patties onto the road. A few hours later, another slips and spills the beer it's been carrying. The local newspaper headline reads "Red meat and beer clogged major traffic arteries Tuesday, slowing the morning commute." No one is injured.

The International Criminal Court, established in 1998, holds its first trial.

Both Grindr and Bitcoin debut.

2009

THE B-SIDE: BURGUNDY'S NEW PRODUCERS

Burgundy is a nearly impossible place to start a business as a young winemaker. For this reason, only a few wineries have come to market over the past twenty years, and almost never in the famed towns of Vosne-Romanée, Chambolle-Musigny, Meursault, and Puligny-Montrachet. Instead, new producers looked to areas and grapes that were considered less than ideal for a long time. One upside of global warming is that these neighboring zones can now produce grapes of a quality akin to the villages that were considered the best sites for centuries. Combine a young and motivated winemaker with more affordable land and a run of good vintages, and you get one of the most exciting times for new Burgundy pretty much ever.

Many of these producers are making wine in a slightly different style, leaning more natural with reds that are paler in color and whites that are saltier in flavor. Other offerings are more classic-minded, reminiscent of the time these producers spent working at some of the best historic wineries, such as Chandon de Briailles, d'Angerville, and Roulot. Many have also taken a liking to the once underwhelming grape, aligote, the other white grape of Burgundy, which had been made into wine without much care. It may be that aligote's low cost has spurred its revolution rather than its potential for greatness, but in the hands of many of these producers, it is undoubtedly delicious. This "B-side" is high quality and still unknown—but bound to hit prime time soon.

Along with the aforementioned producers, a new generation of winemakers has taken over, and they are shifting names to cult status that have never been considered as such before. Here's who to look for:

White Burgundy

Arnaud Ente
Boisson-Vadot
Chanterêves
Domaine Bachelet-Monnot
Domaine de Cassiopée
Domaine de Villaine
Domaine Dureuil-Janthial
Domaine Henri Germain et Fils
Domaine Hubert Lamy
Domaine Lamy-Caillat
Domaine Paul Pillot
Maison Valette
Pierre-Yves Colin-Morey
Vincent Dancer

Red Burgundy

Charles Lachaux
Domaine Berthaut-Gerbet
Domaine des Croix
Domaine Didier Fornerol
Domaine Duroché
Domaine Les Horées
Jean-Marc Vincent
Maison MC Thiriet
Sylvain Pataille

CHABLIS AND CHARLEMAGNE

A VINTAGE LIKE 2010 IS FLAWLESS NEARLY EVERYWHERE. FOR WHITE Burgundy, where chardonnay is the primary grape, it's noted as one of the greatest of all time—especially considering the frequent challenges for the white wine vineyards to come (see page 190). Two heroes of this marvelous year express the opposite ends of Burgundy's spectrum as a region, from the sharp, salty style of the Chablis region to the thick, rich wines of the Corton-Charlemagne vineyard. Those heroes are, respectively, Vincent Dauvissat and Coche-Dury.

Chablis is the crispest and saltiest version of chardonnay made anywhere, standing in contrast to the denser style of wines made in more classic zones of Burgundy, like Meursault, Puligny-Montrachet, and Chassagne-Montrachet. The grape's inherent flavors were compounded by the vintage, making 2010 a legendary Chablis—and the best of the bunch is Vincent Dauvissat Chablis Grand Cru Les Preuses. Until quite recently, Chablis grappled with a reputation for commercial and simple wines—but France's answer to pinot grigio, Vincent Dauvissat's approach, was anything but easy. Dauvissat's wines are like a minimalist painting or a Scandinavian chair: quietly elegant, understated, yet of the highest quality and craft. Although Dauvissat has exceptionally well-located vineyards, that's not the only reason their wines have excelled beyond others. Their winemaking approach is more labor-intensive and time-consuming, using oak barrels for aging delicately, while other Chablis producers use stainless-steel tanks enabled with more controls and a faster turnaround from grape to bottle. Dauvissat's approach results in wines that are simultaneously bright in flavor and rich in texture.

Speaking of rich, Domaine Coche-Dury is the white Burgundy equivalent to Patek Philippe watches: smart, scarce, and, in the eyes of its collectors, mythical. As French icons go, the history of Coche is relatively short. The winery was officially started in 1975 after the marriage of Jean-François Coche and Odile Dury, both of whose families had vineyards in and around the town of Meursault. If Coche's name brings one wine to mind, it's the white from his vineyard Corton-Charlemagne, which is the powerhouse of Burgundy white. When chardonnay ripens to the extreme, like it can in Corton-Charlemagne, its sensation can be as rich and full as a red wine. With Coche's magic touch, the end result is a wine expected to have the body of Corton-Charlemagne, but also with a touch of freshness not found from other producers. His style is singular—so when he announced his retirement in 2010, his last white Burgundy vintage, blood was already in the water: skeptics doubted his son Raphael's ability to continue the flawless run of making the most sought-after white wines. Since that 2010 release, the winery's future as the ruler of white wine has been questioned by collectors—and only time will tell how Raphael succeeds, as the wines made under his leadership age.

The massive explosion of an Icelandic volcano creates an ash cloud that leads to the European continent's biggest disruption in air travel since World War II.

Kathryn Bigelow becomes the first woman to win the Academy Award for Best Director, for her work on *The Hurt Locker*. She remains the only woman to win until Chloé Zhao takes the award home for *Nomadland* eleven years later.

When Tunisian fruit seller Mohamed Bouazizi sets himself on fire in December, it is the match that sparks the Tunisian Revolution and the wider Arab Spring over the ensuing months.

2010

#CHENINCHENINCHENIN

CHENIN BEGAN TO POP UP ON WINE LISTS EVERYWHERE IN 2012. A wave of natural-focused producers—whose efforts were supported by some of the world's top sommeliers, like Pascaline Lepeltier—is credited with bringing chenin to the table, and even earning it a popular hashtag. Yes, chenin blanc became a household wine thanks to Instagram. Thankfully, this grape isn't paying for followers; in the hands of the right producers, the hype is real.

Chenin blanc is a white grape from France's Loire Valley. It's found in other parts of the world as well, but *unlike* a slice of pizza (don't @ me, Italy), it lacks character when made in areas away from its origin. Chenin blanc is the sole white grape in the French regions of Saumur, Anjou, Savennières, Vouvray, and Montlouis, among others, which you'll see noted on a label. The chenin from Saumur, Anjou, and Savennières has lots of acidity and subtly salty and nutty flavors, in contrast to the fruity and floral notes associated with other grapes here, like sauvignon blanc. It's different—and in and around 2012, different started to matter. While some Loire producers skew to the extreme end of natural wines—with flavors more comparable to vinegar than to wine—a handful embody the ethos of natural wine, farming organically and adding minimal amounts of sulfur, but produce an end result as magnificent as any white wine out there. In a French region that has no ranking, if one chenin were to rise above the rest, it would be that from Clos Rougeard.

Clos Rougeard is not a new winery, and chenin blanc is not its main endeavor. In fact, Clos Rougeard is better known for being the greatest producer of the Loire Valley's red grape variety, cabernet franc. In the hands of the Foucault family, which owns Clos Rougeard, cab franc is as serious a red as any great wine from Bordeaux or Burgundy, and they're responsible for sparking an international obsession with the grape. It's unique in that it has big flavors like tobacco, dark cherries, and dried chiles, but its taste is as delicate and invigorating as a chilled Beaujolais or lighter syrah. The small amount of chenin blanc they make alongside their red wines is the rarest bottling in their portfolio, made from the century-old vines of their Brezé vineyard in Saumur. Brezé is a grand cru–worthy vineyard for chenin, and white wines bearing "Brezé" on their labels taste broad but not oaky, a rarity among white wines with this power. This is chenin blanc at its highest potential, with the body of Burgundy and flavors that can only be found in the Loire.

Clos Rougeard paved the path for other producers in this region to shine, too. In the mid-'90s Romain Guiberteau was in law school but not thriving when the opportunity arose to take over his family's winery, Domaine Guiberteau. He sought guidance from Nady Foucault of Clos Rougeard for his neighboring vineyards of chenin blanc and cabernet

The Supreme Court agrees to review *United States v. Windsor*, paving the way for the legalization of same-sex marriage three years later.

The final Canadian penny is minted on May 4, after the government announces that one-cent pieces—which cost 1.6 cents to make—will be withdrawn from circulation.

Swiss scientists develop a robot that can be controlled by thoughts alone.

2012

franc. Guiberteau's wines reflect their place in a similar manner as Clos Rougeard's, with rich-but-crisp, savory-but-light whites and reds made famous by his mentor.

It's not uncommon for a winemaker's résumé to be reflected in the taste of their wines throughout history and the world over. An essay on such storied partnerships would be a long one, but for another tale of successful chenin, we look to Stéphane Bernaudeau, who worked for one of the Loire's first natural winemakers, Mark Angeli of Ferme de la Sansonnière, before going out on his own. Bernaudeau makes wine in Anjou, just down the river from the more acclaimed region of Saumur. The area is famous for sweet wine, but the wines from his tiny estate are anything but. In fact, it's best not to have any expectations for Bernaudeau's wines; he's just too avant-garde to be pinned down. His is a style of white wine that has only newly emerged as popular and is now considered blue chip. The wines are natural with a subtle cloudy hue, a not-so-subtle salty taste, and as much acidity as any dry white wine in the world. They're also super rare. Bernaudeau is one of the first natural winemakers to become collectible from the region, and his success can only be compared to the mythical wines of Pierre Overnoy in the Jura or Valentini from Abruzzo. The apex of his range comes from the century-old vines of Les Nourrissons.

WHAT DOES IT MEAN?
NATURAL WINE

If you ask for something other than organic or natural or biodynamic at any hip wine bar these days, you might feel a bit like you're asking for meat at a vegan restaurant. But how many of the people who are sipping cloudy pét-nat actually know the difference between the three categories?

An organic wine is the simplest to define. The term has to do with the farming stage of the winemaking process. Quite simply, if the grapes are grown organically (without chemical fertilizers or pesticides), the wine is organic.

Biodynamic also has to do with the farming stage. Think of it as organic+. In the same way that all citrus are fruit, but not all fruit are citrus, all biodynamic farms are organic, but not all organic farms are biodynamic. To be the latter, you've got to layer a bunch more processes and procedures on top of that organic baseline. (For a lot more on biodynamic wine, see page 142.)

Then you've got natural wine, which is also called "lo-fi," "minimal intervention," or "zero/zero wine" (meaning nothing was added or taken away). Unlike the other two labels, this one has to do with the winemaking part of the process. But if someone tells you they know exactly what a natural wine is, they're lying. The term has no legal definition, and no accrediting body exists. Generally speaking, it's an organic grape that gets turned into wine using as little intervention as possible. No added yeast. Little to no temperature control. No added enzymes or preservatives like sulfur. No filtration. Winemakers can get extreme here. Some producers specify that the grapes must be plucked and destemmed by hand. Others say that "whole cluster" is the way to go, in which stems are left on during the fermenting process, adding a kind of spice to the final product.

You can find many beautiful natural wines, and as the movement grows and matures, that's only becoming truer. But minimal isn't easy, and wine can get really weird really fast. So don't feel bad if you don't like a certain natural wine—and know that it doesn't mean you dislike all natural wine.

BURLOTTO BOOSTS BAROLO

THE ERA OF OLD-SCHOOL BAROLO THAT STARTED IN THE 1940s WAS shaken up in the '90s by a change in tastes toward fruitier, bigger, international-style wines. Many wineries in the region fell into one camp or the other—traditional or modern. A criticism of some traditional wines is that they required too much time to become gentle enough to drink (see page 93), while modern wines lacked the tannins needed to keep them fresh and uniquely Barolo-flavored. Thankfully, in the early aughts, a shift in taste struck a balance between both worlds. It respected the old-guard flavors, but embraced the changing weather and its ability to make wines ready to drink younger.

G. B. Burlotto emerged as a star through this transition. Burlotto had long been making wine in Verduno, which is the highest altitude—and therefore coolest part—of Barolo. Their vineyard, Monvigliero, is an exceptional site, but it was largely unknown except among the most passionate Italian drinkers. That all changed when wine critic Antonio Galloni awarded Burlotto's 2013 vintage 100 points. Whatever might have been considered a 100-point Barolo ten years prior, Burlotto's wine was the opposite. Made using generations-old techniques, like stomping the grapes by foot and whole cluster fermenting to gently extract flavors, it was a one-of-a-kind Barolo whose flavors reflected both Burlotto's hand and the vineyard's delicate characteristics. Burlotto had been making wine this way for decades, but critics had not yet favored the style. So when this intensely aromatic, lean, and delicate wine received 100 points, the Barolo community—including the winemaker himself—was shocked. But it's deserving of the praise, as it showcases Barolo's ability to make wines of finesse rather than power. Producers across the region have increasingly looked to Burlotto as a prime example of how to simultaneously maintain tradition and adapt to an ever-changing environment.

Other great producers seeking elegance in Barolo are:

- Brovia
- Cantina d'Arcy
- Cantina del Pino
- Cavallotto
- Ferdinando Principiano
- Lalù
- Olek Bondonio
- Philine Isabelle
- Roagna
- Trediberri

Uruguay becomes the first country to legalize weed.

China relaxes its one-child policy in response to a rapidly aging population and the country's low male-to-female ratio. The policy officially ends in 2016.

A huge meteor explodes without warning over the Russian city of Chelyabinsk, injuring more than one thousand residents. Scientists begin developing a Spaceguard to protect Earth from extraterrestrial fly balls.

2013

PROTECT THE NORTH: ALTO PIEMONTE

Alto Piemonte refers to the small regions in the northern part of Piemonte, the Italian province encompassing villages like Barolo and Barbaresco. Around the beginning of the twentieth century, Alto Piemonte, which most notably includes the zones of Gattinara, Caremma, Lessona, and Bramaterra, had almost one hundred times the number of planted vineyards that it does today. Over the ensuing decades, due to financial hardships and a flight of workers to the Fiat factory in the nearby city of Torino, that volume of winemaking became increasingly unsustainable. Only recently has the promise of a stable wine industry in the area seemed plausible again, thanks in large part to the international success of Barolo, as well as to a small group of quality-minded producers in the area. Like in Barolo, the primary grape in the subregion is nebbiolo, but the region is even higher in altitude and lower in temperature. So, similar to the style of Burlotto, the wines of Alto Piemonte are delicate and lighter in body, while maintaining the dramatic aromas and flavors of the best nebbiolo. Its potential has been recognized by one of Barolo's best and most ambitious winemakers, Roberto Conterno of Giacomo Conterno, who acquired the Nervi winery in Gattinara in 2018. A few other wineries have been at it for a while but only recently began buzzing again.

Drink these if you're looking for some of the best value in Italian wine today:

- Antoniolo in Gattinara
- Cristiano Garella in Bramaterra
- Ferrando in Carema
- Le Pianelle in Bramaterra
- Proprietà Sperino in Lessona

THE UNLUCKY SEVEN

UNLIKE A MUSIC TRACK OR A LIMITED-RELEASE H+M DESIGNER COLlection, winemakers rarely collaborate. That's not to say they're opposed to doing so, but a harvest is usually something each producer has to endure individually. Only recently, in response to increasingly difficult harvests as a result of climate change, have some of the world's best winemakers begun to look at other countries and hemispheres to diversify their holdings, leading to joint ventures only possible with harvests that don't run concurrently. That said, 2016 was the exception.

In 2016, Burgundy experienced one of the most vicious frosts of all time. Frost in March and April, the early part of the season, is the worst. The vines are just starting to bud, and frost stunts the growth of the shoot that eventually bears the fruit, which means the shoot won't produce grapes that season. It's like losing all your money at the poker table on your first hand of cards, with no chance to buy back in.

That year, none of the seven different owners of Montrachet, the most expensive and exclusive white wine vineyard in the world, had enough grapes to make the wines that are individually the gems of their respective portfolios. So they did the unthinkable: they came together to bottle a single wine. Even combined, the grapes produced only six hundred bottles under the name L'Exceptionnelle Vendange des 7 Domaines ("The Exceptional Harvest of 7 Wineries"). Legally, this collaboration was possible since all of Montrachet is planted with chardonnay; in essence, the raw material of each individual property was identical.

The frost didn't only impact volume, however. While the 2016 vintage is famed for its collaboration and scarcity, it's not necessarily remembered for its taste. The leading winemaker from Domaine Leflaive said that while the effort was something to be proud of, "We hope, however, to never have to do this again." That's a direct quote.

Here's an accounting of the seven Montrachet producers of 2016, including how many bottles they got to sell that year:

- Claudine Petitjean: 45 bottles, compared to 300 normally
- Domaine de la Romanée-Conti: 280 bottles, compared to 3,000 normally
- Domaine des Comtes Lafon: 139 bottles, compared to 2,400 normally
- Domaine Fleurot-Larose: 46 bottles, compared to 300 normally
- Domaine Guy Amiot: 71 bottles, compared to 600 normally
- Domaine Lamy-Pillot: 45 bottles, compared to 300 normally
- Domaine Leflaive: 57 bottles, compared to 300 normally

Twenty-eight swimmers become the first to cross the inhospitably salty Dead Sea to raise awareness of the body of water's imminent risk of becoming extinct.

Lin-Manuel Miranda's *Hamilton* wins the Tony Award for Best Musical, unleashing poor karaoke choices for years to come.

The United Kingdom votes to leave the EU, Trump wins the US presidency, and the augmented reality game *Pokémon GO* helps us all escape.

2016

CELEBRATING THE FRENCH UNDERDOGS

THE JURA, A FRENCH ALPINE REGION NOT FAR FROM BURGUNDY, IS primarily known as a natural wine region, but it deserves to be included in the canon of the world's most respected overall. Entire books have been devoted to its history, and even to its soil. The Jura is very much its own place, and its wines have their own voice, whether sparkling, white, red, or sweet. The white grapes are chardonnay and savagnin, two grapes that have similar textures and flavors, while the reds—pinot noir, trousseau, and the less common poulsard—are usually bottled on their own. Both the whites and the reds are commonly compared to their counterparts in Burgundy, and for good reason, as the two regions share a lot stylistically.

Despite this history, the area's best producers only started to become celebrities in the wine world in 2017. There was no collective marketing strategy. The public simply began to recognize that the Jura puts out truly great wine, reaffirming, in a broader sense, that consumers were no longer chasing the big wines of the '90s but were all in on the lean ones of today.

The success of the Jura came from a wave of producers who, early on, believed in their region. Domaine Pierre Overnoy is the most avant-garde and important producer in the history of the Jura. After Overnoy, Ganevat was the next Jura producer to gain cult status. Ganevat blends vintages and grapes and utilizes various winemaking techniques to produce an extraordinary, albeit confusing, range of wines. Domaine Tissot, a great entry point into the Jura, also makes a huge range of wines, from affordable sparkling to rare single vineyards, that demonstrates the vastness of this area. The white wines are saline and rich, while the reds are wild and light. And before Jacques Puffeney sold his vineyards and retired in 2014, his wines were a gateway to the Jura for many in the American market—subtly earthy but still precise, always affordable, and always compelling. This OG group mentored the newest generation. The new kids, some deservedly and others just because they are a new name, have quickly become the icons of the region, often overshadowing the original Jura producers.

It's possible that the best wine in the Jura is currently from Japanese winemaker Kenjirō Kagami of Domaines des Miroirs. Kagami strikes a balance between natural and classic wines. His inaugural vintage was 2011, and due to their scarcity, his wines have since become some of France's most sought-after.

Similar to Miroirs, the work of the late Pascal Clairet combines great wine with tiny quantities, resulting in a winery whose reputation is

2017

mammoth despite its minuscule size. Clairet's wines are some of the greatest examples of the Jura's unique quality. Though they follow the playbook of natural wine, as most in the Jura do, labeling them as "natural" would be reductive. In the hands of such a talented winemaker, they are pure rather than wild and obscure. Other natural but classic wines include Domaine des Murmures, whose wines are tasty, straightforward, and uncertain—in a good way—and Étienne Thiebaud's Domaine des Cavarodes. The former, established in 2012, has already hit the auction market with force, and some are betting on it as if it's a varsity basketball player destined to be the next LeBron. For the moment, though, you can still enjoy Murmures's wines at their affordable release price without paying big league prices. The latter has quickly become respected as one of the Jura's best producers. Thiebaud founded the winery after working at the Jura legend Domaine de la Tournelle, and wines from Cavarodes have a similarly clean and crisp style as Tournelle's.

And then there are the super naturals. If you're looking for a shock, seek out Jura producers who make natural wines not only free of added sulfur, but also free of caring about meeting any expectations.

———————

Natural wines push boundaries of flavors, and these producers are the ones to look for—or look out for, if that isn't your thing. The list includes:

- Domaine de l'Octavin
- Les Dolomies
- Peggy and Jean-Pascal Buronfosse
- Philippe Bornard
- Renaud Bruyère and Adeline Houillon

NO WAY: ROSÉ

It would be more than fair to say that in the past five to ten years, the rosé industry has been having a moment. It's become the business venture of everyone from housewives to Post Malone. And it's made its way into cans, bags, and even frozen drink machines. That's all to say, somewhere along the way, rosé lost its focus on, well, being a wine. There's no shame in that game, but it's worth underlining that rosé has long since transitioned from the pale pink drink of Southern France to a category of alcohol all on its own.

Most are made conventionally (meaning identically), so it doesn't really matter whether they're from Provence or Long Island—they all taste nearly the same. But that's no reason not to fill your glass with rosé. Enjoying a cold glass of any alcohol on a hot summer day is pretty nice. Rosé is easy to drink, too—no need to swirl and sniff. Just throw it back and make sure there's none left in the cellar (or, more likely, the fridge) after Labor Day.

If you *are* looking to class up your rosé experience, some producers do farm organically, and take care to turn out a better product than what the masses consume. Rosé is made around the globe, and delicious examples can be found in almost every corner.

Reach for these dry and ultra-thirst-quenching bottles:

- Ameztoi Txakolina Rosado (Basque Country, Spain)
- Clos Cibonne Rosé (Provence, France)
- Domaine Tempier Bandol Rosé (Bandol, France)
- Domaine Vacheron Rosé (Sancerre, France)
- Girolamo Russo Etna Rosato (Sicily, Italy)
- Matthiasson Rosé (Northern California, US)
- Stein Rosé (Mosel, Germany)

MEUNIER MAKES THE TEAM

AROUND 2018, CHAMPAGNE, ONE OF THE WORLD'S OLDEST COMMERCIAL wine regions, firmly entered into its next phase. The grower Champagne movement, which started in the late '80s with a group of small businesses making wine from grapes they farmed on their own land (see page 124), had matured to the point that it had classic producers as well as a wave of newbies. Names like Pierre Peters and their benchmark Les Chetillons bottling (made from 100 percent chardonnay) had become collectibles alongside Krug, Cristal, and Dom Pérignon. And the success of Selosse, who had led the charge for this movement over the previous few decades, gave way to the likes of Jérôme Prévost, who got his start by borrowing space in Selosse's winery.

Prévost's grape of choice is meunier. Wine pros assign stigma to certain grapes: pinot grigio is weak, merlot is boring, and, once upon time, pinot meunier was always picked last. Pinot meunier is the third grape of Champagne, ranked below the more lauded chardonnay and pinot noir. It had been planted abundantly around the region in the postwar era because it was easier to grow, but it was most commonly used as a blending grape. Prévost set out to change all that, and used pinot meunier to make both his rosé and classic Champagnes, which are among the highest-quality bubbles today. He exclusively makes vintage wines, but their year is never obvious; legally, he doesn't age them long enough to put the year on the label. But you can find the year if you know where to look: next to the letters *LC* on the bottle. For example, "LC18" denotes that the wine is made entirely with grapes from the 2018 vintage. Others, including Aurélien Lurquin, Chartogne-Taillet, Egly-Ouriet, Emmanuel Brochet, and Georges Laval, have since been encouraged by Prévost's risk-taking with meunier and bottled some of their own. The grape has finally earned the respect it deserves.

Following the poisoning of a former Russian spy and his daughter with the lethal nerve agent Novichok, a remarkable public health official named Tracy Daszkiewicz leads a cleanup effort that prevents a catastrophe in Salisbury, England.

After being trapped in a cave in Thailand for seventeen days, twelve boys and their soccer coach are saved thanks to a rescue operation that requires professional divers and lots of anesthesia.

A study published in the science journal *Nature* reveals that all varieties of citrus trace their origins to the foothills of the Himalayas.

2018

SPAIN SINGS

For several decades, Spain's wine was suffering an identity crisis. Many Spanish reds tried to taste American-made—that is, big and highly alcoholic. (It's the same story that gave rise to boozy bottles in Italy and parts of France: pulling for points came at the cost of celebrating the wineries' unique characteristics.) While this style saw some successes, like the long-lived wines of Vega Sicilia, Spanish reds were by and large boring. As for white wines, those that made it out of the country at all were chasing the successes of easy-drinkers like sauvignon blanc and pinot grigio rather than daring to compete with the more distinguished white wines of Burgundy (which Spanish whites have since proven they certainly can—and often do—outperform). Recently, Spain's wines have found themselves again, and this time, salvation came from middle-of-nowhere vineyards scattered throughout the country's islands, mountains, and coasts, rather than the more common regions of Ribera del Duero, Rioja, and Priorat.

As of 2020, Spain and neighboring Portugal may, in fact, be the world's most exciting region. The wines being celebrated are those that doubled down on their own flavors in lieu of the international style. They come mostly from grapes not found anywhere else that yield the savory, saltier, lighter styles that are now the most sought-after. The producers who have been foundational in this Spanish shift are all start-ups of sorts. They're people who fell in love with wine, found some affordable vineyards, and happened to be talented. In short order, they have made wine the world has fallen in love with, too.

The best of Spain today comes from these producers:

- Comando G
- Envinate
- Goyo García Viadero
- Laura Lorenzo
- Luis Rodriguez
- Nanclares y Prieto
- Raúl Pérez

Sourdough. Banana bread. Whipped coffee. Scallion regeneration on windowsills. Matching sweatsuits. *Tiger King.* We were . . . going through some shit—and unfortunately, toilet paper was a scarcity.

Speaking of the abyss: astronomers announce the discovery of the first black hole in a part of the universe visible to the naked eye.

And as a tiny silver lining, scientists observe an unprecedented healing of the ozone hole during the (first) COVID lockdown period.

2020

ACKNOWLEDGMENTS

Drinking and talking about wine is easy; putting that to paper is not. Thank you to Chris Stang whose excellent writing and guidance on our book, *How to Drink Wine,* not only gave me the confidence to write this book, but has also been a source of continued inspiration for my other endeavors.

Thank you to Amanda Englander, the editor of both that book and this one, who not only gave me the opportunity, but also dragged me to the finish line, and whose exceptional skill and organization took my words and turned them into prose.

Thanks to Becky Cooper for collaborating on this book with me. Her wit, diligence, and exceptional writing of the timelines and select sidebars inspired the tone of this book and made it a work of both wine and of culture at large.

Thank you to Ian Dingman and Joan Wong, whose creativity and craftsmanship helped make a wine book that looks so special and distinctive. This book wouldn't be the same without their work.

Thank you to the UNSQ team for their support and patience in ensuring we published an excellent book, especially to Caroline Hughes, Melissa Farris, Lisa Forde, Linda Liang, Jennifer Halper, Kevin Iwano, and Lindsay Herman. And thanks to Terry Deal, Ivy McFadden, and Alison Skrabek for ensuring its accuracy as well.

Thank you to my team at Parcelle, especially to my partner, Josh Abramson, who picked up my slack while I wrote this book. Thanks to Matt Tervooren and Matthew Mather who read and edited many early and very rough versions of this text. Thank you especially to Arvid Rosengren, my friend and partner, who is the most studious (and calmest) wine person I know.

Without the generosity, patience, and wisdom that has been shared so openly with me by some, I never would have found a career in wine, let alone one writing about it. I wrote this book based on notes, emails, and memories that I've made with winemakers, collectors, importers, and sommeliers, who are great friends and even better people.

Thank you to my former employers and mentors, Bobby Stuckey and Lachlan Mackinnon-Patterson, for giving me a job in wine when I was just twenty-one years old and didn't know how to tie a tie. Thanks to Hugo Matheson and Kimbal Musk at The Kitchen for unknowingly allowing me to attend wine classes before I should have. And to David Nicola of Mr. Mike's Pizza in Lake Placid, New York, who is the most optimistic and generous restaurant guy I've ever met.

To Robert Bohr, to whom I will forever be grateful: one of my best friends, mentors, and favorite people to drink a few bottles of wine with. His hard work, generosity, and knowledge changed my life, and many others', too.

Thank you to my family for the encouragement to do what I love. It gave me the confidence to follow that path.

REFERENCES AND FURTHER LEARNING

Broadbent, Michael. *Michael Broadbent's Vintage Wine.*
London: Harcourt/Webster's International, 2002.

Dalton, Levi, host. *I'll Drink to That* (podcast),
Anticipation Audio Co., 2012–, www.illdrinktothatpod.com.

Feiring, Alice. *Natural Wine for the People.*
Emeryville, CA: Ten Speed Press, 2019.

Galloni, Antonio. Vinous Media (website), vinous.com.

Keeling, Dan, and Mark Andrew. *Noble Rot* magazine, 2013–.

Liem, Peter. *Champagne Guide* (blog),
www.champagneguide.net.

Morris, Jasper. *Inside Burgundy.*
London: Berry Bros & Rudd Press, 2010.

O'Keefe, Kerin. *Barolo and Barbaresco.*
Oakland, CA: University of California Press, 2014.

Parker, Robert. *The Wine Advocate* magazine, 1978–.

Parr, Rajat, and Jordan Mackay. *Secret of the Sommeliers.*
Emeryville, CA: Ten Speed Press, 2010.

Sohm, Aldo. *Wine Simple.*
New York: Clarkson Potter, 2019.

INDEX

A

Aglianico, 87
Alicante bouschet grape, 51
Aligote grape, 178
Allemand, Thierry, 137
Alsace, 117
Alto Piemonte, 188
American Viticulture Area
    (AVA) system, 108–9
Angeli, Mark, 184
Anjou, 184
Appellation d'Origine Protégée
    (AOP) system, 108–9
Australian wine, 68

B

Barbaresco, 80, 84
Barolo, 72, 79, 80, 93, 152, 187
Bartolo Mascarello, 72
Bâtonnage, 167
Beaujolais, 111
Beaujolais Nouveau, 111
Beaulieu Vineyard, 54
Benanti family, 155
Bernaudeau, Stéphane, 184
Biodynamic farming, 59, 140,
    142–43, 145, 185

Bize-Leroy, Lalou, 140
Blanc de Blancs, 124
Bolgheri, 87
Bonaparte, Napoleon, 23
Bordeaux
    1855 rankings, 23
    2003 vintage, 161
    Château Margaux, 29
    iconic postwar vintages,
        61
    Left Bank, 64, 114
    Right Bank, 64, 114
Bordeaux Wine Official
    Classification of 1855, 23
Breg, 149
Brezé vineyard, 183
Brunello, 163–64
Brunello di Montalcino, 168
Burgundy
    1934 Richebourg Vieux
        Cépages, 48
    1937 Lafarge, 53
    1959 Rousseau, 76
    1969 vintage, 90
    2004 vintage, 163
    2016 frost conditions, 190
    biodynamic farming in, 145
    Burgundy-like wines from
        California, 118
    Clos des Ducs, 36
    Cros Parantoux, 101
    generational vineyards, 177
    Grand Cru of Musigny, 67
    label names, 123
    land and sun variations, 158
    new producers, 178–79
    transition to organic
        farming, 140

    white, in 2010, 180
    wine classifications, 38
Burlotto, G. B., 187

C

Cabernet franc, 87, 183
Cabernet sauvignon, 87
California winemakers, 48, 54,
    83, 90, 98, 118
Cantina Mascarello, 72
Case Basse, 168
Celebrity-endorsed wines, 175
Celebrity winemakers, 59
Cerasuolo, 156
Chablis, 105, 180
Chambertin vineyard, 35
Champagne
    Blanc de Blanc, 124
    blending technique, 32
    Champagne Salon, 30
    Dom Pérignon, 41, 76
    grower Champagne
        movement, 197
    importers, 126
    Krug Grand Cuvée, 171
    multi-vintage (MV), 32
    non-vintage (NV), 32
    pinot meunier for, 197
    rosé, 76
    Substance, 124

Vieilles Vignes Françaises, 27
Chardonnay, 97, 105, 106
Charles Krug winery, 83
Château d'Yquem, 18
Château-Grillet, 138
Château Haut-Brion, 71, 131
Château Lafite, 17
Château Lafleur, 114
Château Margaux, 29
Chateau Montelena, 97
Château Mouton Rothschild, 67, 114
Chateau Musar, 76
Châteauneuf-du-Pape, 127–28
Château Rayas, 128
Chenin blanc, 94, 183
Cheval Blanc, 64
Chianti, 102
Chianti Classico, 88
Chianti PDO, 108
Clairet, Pascal, 193–94
Climate change, 161, 165, 175
Clos de la Roche, 123
Clos des Ducs vineyard, 36
Clos Rougeard, 183
Clos Sainte Hune, 117
Clos Saint-Jacques, 76
Coates' Law of Maturity, 62
Coche, François, 180
Cold vintages, 163
Condrieu, 138
Consulting winemakers, 135
Conterno, Roberto, 188
Conterno family, 105
Corks, 167
Cork taint, 21, 167
Cornas, 137
Cornelissen, Frank, 155
Corton-Charlemagne vineyard, 180
Cros Parantoux, 101
Cuvée Cathelin, 137

D

D'Angerville, Guillaume, 36
D'Angerville, Sem, 36
Dauvissat, Vincent, 180
Denominazione di Origine Controllata (DOC), 109
Denominazione di Origine Controllata e Garantita (DOCG), 109
Diam, 21
Domaine Auguste Clape, 128
Domaine Coche-Dury, 180
Domaine Comte Georges de Vogüé, 67
Domaine de la Romanée-Conti (DRC), 42, 48, 61, 140
Domaine des Cavarodes, 194
Domaine des Murmures, 194
Domaine Georges Mugneret, 177
Domaine Georges Mugneret-Gibourg, 177
Domaine Georges Roumier, 67
Domaine Guiberteau, 183–84
Domaine Jean-Louis Chave, 137, 138
Domaine Leflaive, 106, 145
Domaine Leroy, 140
Domaine Mugneret-Gibourg, 177
Domaine Pierre Overnoy, 193
Domaine Ponsot, 123
Domaine Roulot, 97
Domaines des Miroirs, 193
Domaine Tissot, 193
Dom Pérignon, 41, 76
Draper, Paul, 90
Dury, Odile, 180

E

Electrodialysis, 165
Engel, René, 163

F

Farming methods, 59, 111, 140, 142–43, 145, 185
Fortified wines, 46–47
Foti, Salvo, 155
Foucault, Nady, 183
Foucault family, 183
French wine importers, 126
Friuli, 149, 156

G

Gaja, Angelo, 84
Ganevat, 193
Gaudichots, 42
German wine importers, 126
Gevrey-Chambertin, 76
Giacomo Conterno, 188
Giacomo Conterno Monfortino, 105
Giacosa, Bruno, 80
Gibourg, Jeanne, 177

Giuseppe Mascarello Barolo
  Monprivato, 93
Grand Cru Classés en 1855,
  23
Grand Cru of Musigny, 67
Grand Cuvée, 171
Grange, 68
Grape bricks, 51
Graves, 71, 131
Gravner, Josko, 149, 150
Great Comet of 1811, 18
Grower Champagne
  movement, 197
Guigal winery, 123

Italian winemakers, 72, 84, 87,
  102
Italian wines, 152, 155

J

Jayer, Henri, 101
Jefferson, Thomas, 17
Jeroboam, 74
Joly, Nicolas, 94
Judgment of Paris, 97
Jura region, 117, 193–94

H

Harlan, 146
Haut-Brion, 71, 131
Heat, 161, 165
Heitz Cellar Martha's
  Vineyard, 98
Heitz, Joe, 98
Hermitage Blanc, 137, 138
Hermitage Rouge, 137
Hochar, Serge, 76

K

Kabinett, 94
Kagami, Kenjirō, 193
Koch, Bill, 17
Krankl, Manfred, 146
Krug, 171

I

Importers, 126
Italian wine importers, 126

L

Labels, on wine, 114
La Chapelle, 79

La Coulée de Serrant vineyard,
  94
Lafarge, Michel, 53
Lafarge wines, 53
Lafite Rothschild winery, 171
La Mission Haut-Brion, 71
Lapierre, Marcel, 111
La Romanée vineyard, 158
La Tâche vineyard, 42, 158
Latour, Georges de, 54
Laville Haut-Brion, 94
Lebanon, 76
Leflaive, Anne-Claude, 143,
  145
Le Montrachet vineyard, 106
Le Pergole Torte, 102
Leroy family, 140
L'Exceptionnelle Vendange
  des 7 Domaines, 190
Liger-Belair, Just, 158
Liger-Belair, Louis-Michel, 158
Liger-Belair, Michel, 158
Liger-Belair family, 42, 158
Loire Valley, 94, 183
López de Heredia, Rafael, 24
López de Heredia winery, 24
Lunar cycles, 142

M

Madeira, 46
Magnum, 74
Maison Leroy, 140
Marketing methods, 146, 171
Martha's Vineyard (vineyard),
  98
Mascarello, Maria Teresa, 72
Mascarello family, 93

Mastroberardino winery, 87
Médoc, 71
Meunier, 197
Meyer, Eugène, 143
Miani, 156
Moët & Chandon, 41
Mondavi, Robert, 83
Monfortino, 105
Monprivato, 93
Montalcino, 164
Monte Bello, 90
Montepulciano, 155–56
Montevertine winery, 102
Montrachet, 106, 190
Montrachet vineyard, 145
Monvigliero vineyard, 187
Morey, Pierre, 106
Mount Etna, 155
Mouton Rothschild, 67, 114
Mugneret, André, 177
Mugneret, Georges, 177
Mugneret, Marie-Andrée, 177
Mugneret, Marie-Cristine, 177
Müller, Egon, 94
Musigny vineyard, 67

N

Napa Valley, 145
Natural fermentation, 111
Natural wine importers, 126
Natural wines, 117, 168, 183, 185, 194
Nebuchadnezzar, 74
Négociants, 36
Nerello grape, 155
Noble rot, 47

O

Orange wine, 149, 150
Oregon pinot noir, 120
Organic farming, 59, 111, 140, 142, 185
Overnoy, Pierre, 117
Oxidation, 117, 166–67

P

Parker, Robert, 114, 134–35, 145, 161
Paul Jaboulet Aîné winery, 79
Pérignon, Dom Pierre, 41
Peterson, Heidi, 145
Philips, Jean, 145
Phylloxera, 24, 26–27, 45
Piemonte, 188
Pietramarina, 155
Pinault, François, 163
Pinot grigio, 157
Pinot meunier, 197
Pinot noir, 118, 120
Point system, 134–35
Ponsot, Laurent, 123
Pontoni, Enzo, 156
Portugal, 45, 198
Port wine, 45
Premox, 166–67
Prévost, Jérôme, 197
Prohibition, 48, 50–51
Protected designation of origin (PDO), 108
Puffeney, Jacques, 193

Q

Queen of Spades, 146
Quinta do Noval Nacional, 45

R

Ramonet, Pierre, 106
Raveneau Chablis, 105
Rhône Valley, 127, 137, 138
Richebourg Vieux Cépages, 48
Ridge Vineyards, 90
Riesling, 94, 117
Riley, Charles Valentine, 26–27
Rioja, 24
Rocchetta, Incisa della, 87
Rocchetta, Marchese Mario Incisa della, 87
Rolland, Michel, 135
Romain Guiberteau, 183
Rosé, 76, 150, 156, 195
Roulot, 97
Roumier, Georges, 67
Rousseau, Armand, 76
Rousseau family, 35
Rovittello, 155

S

Saint-Émilion winery, 64
Salmanazar, 74

Salon, Eugène-Aimé, 30
Sangiovese, 163
Sangiovese-only Chianti, 102
Santo Stefano Riserva, 80
Sassicaia, 87, 135
Sauternes, 18
Sauvignon blanc, 94
Scharzhof vineyard, 94
Schubert, Max, 68
Screaming Eagle, 145
Selosse, 197
Selosse, Anselme, 124
Selyem, Ed, 118
Serra della Contessa, 155
Seysses, Jacques, 90
Sherry, 46
Sherry-making method, 32
Shiraz, 68
Sine Qua Non (SQN), 146
Smooth (wine description), 152
Social media, 174
Soldera, Gianfranco, 168
Solera method, 32, 124
Sori San Lorenzo, 84
Spanish wine, 198
Steiner, Rudolf, 142, 143
Substance, 124
Sulfur, in wine, 112
Super Tuscans, 88
Sweet wines, 46–47
Syrah, 123, 137

Trebbiano, 155–56
Trimbach family, 117
Trockenbeerenauslese, 94
Tuscany, 88, 152

V

Valentini, 155–56
Vega Sicilia, 198
Vendange tardive, 117
Ventura County, 146
Verset, Noël, 137
Vincent Dauvissat Chablis
    Grand Cru Les Preuses, 180
Vin de France, 109
Vin jaune, 117
Viognier grape, 138
Volstead Act, 50

T

Taurasi, 87
Tchelistcheff, André, 54
Thiebaud, Étienne, 194
Tokaji, 47

changing trends, 175
classification systems,
    134–35
commercialization of, 14–15
"estate" or "domaine," 38
fortified, 46–47
importers, 126
import market, 58–59
labels, 114
natural wines, 117, 168, 183,
    185, 194
orange wine, 149, 150
origins of, 14
peak maturity, 62
point system, 134–35
poorly aged and spoiled, 62
progression, at dinners, 105
regional laws, 108–9
"single-vineyard," 38
storage, 20–21
table wines, 87, 102
yellow wine, 117
Wine Advocate newsletter, 134
World War II, 53, 58

W

White Bordeaux, 94
"White-label" model, 140
White wines, 94, 106, 117, 131,
    138, 166–67
Williams, Burt, 118
Williams Selyem wines, 118
Wine
    bottle sizes and names, 74
    boxed, 21
    celebrity-endorsed, 175

Y

Yellow wine, 117

UNION SQUARE & CO.

NEW YORK

UNION SQUARE & CO. and the distinctive Union Square & Co. logo
are trademarks of Sterling Publishing Co., Inc.

Union Square & Co., LLC, is a subsidiary of Sterling Publishing Co., Inc.

ISBN 978-1-4549-4750-9
ISBN 978-1-4549-4751-6 (e-book)

For information about custom editions, special sales, and premium
purchases, please contact specialsales@unionsquareandco.com.

Printed in China

2 4 6 8 10 9 7 5 3 1

unionsquareandco.com

Editor: Amanda Englander
Art Director: Ian Dingman
Creative Director: Melissa Farris
Illustrator: Joan Wong
Production Editor: Lindsay Herman
Copy Editor: Terry Deal
Production Manager: Kevin Iwano
Proofreaders: Ivy McFadden, Alison Skrabek
Indexer: Elizabeth Parson

Cover image courtesy of Rare Book Division, the New York Public
Library. *Vitis laciniata = Vigne laciniée*, the New York Public Library
Digital Collections, 1801–1819.

Images courtesy of: Biodiversity Heritage Library, Internet Archive,
Library of Congress, Metropolitan Museum of Art, NASA, National
Gallery of Art, New York Public Library, Pexels, Poland State Archives,
Smithsonian Institution, Unsplash, Wikimedia Commons
Additional images: iStock/Getty Images Plus